HELP® 2

Handbook of Exercises for Language Processing

Authors:
Andrea M. Lazzari
Patricia Myers Peters

Volume 2
Specific Word Finding
Categorization
Wh-Questions
Grammar

Problem / Skill Area:	Language
Interest Level:	1st grade thru Adult
Reading Level:	1.5 thru 2.5

Copyright © 1987 LinguiSystems, Inc.

Limited Reproduction Allowed

LinguiSystems grants to individual teachers and other professionals the limited right to reproduce and distribute copies of these worksheets for noncommercial, face-to-face individual, group or classroom instruction. All copies must include LinguiSystems' copyright notice.

Reproduction and distribution of these worksheets for an entire school, school system or group of professionals is strictly prohibited.

LinguiSystems

LinguiSystems, Inc.
3100 4th Avenue
East Moline, IL 61244

1-800-PRO IDEA
1-800-776-4332

Printed in U.S.A.
ISBN 1-55999-181-X

About the Authors

Andrea M. Lazzari, Ed. D., is a private educational consultant in Richmond, Virginia. She has worked as a speech-language pathologist in the public schools, in a community clinic, and in private practice for a total of eight years. She has also been a teacher of preschool handicapped students and the Supervisor of Early Childhood Special Education Programs for the state of Virginia. In addition to co-authoring the *HELP* series for LinguiSystems, Andrea is also the author of *Just for Adults*.

Patricia Myers Peters, M. Ed., CCC is employed as a speech-language pathologist by Rehabilitation Services of Roanoke, Inc., Roanoke, Virginia. She works with a communicatively disordered population ranging from preschool through geriatric ages.

Andrea and Patricia have co-authored nine publications in the *HELP* series with LinguiSystems since 1980.

August 1991

Dedication

This book is respectfully dedicated to Russell Murphy and the Reverend Curtis Robertson.

Table of Contents

Introduction..5

Specific Word Finding
     Contents..7
     Tasks...8
     General Activities.................................25

Categorization
     Contents...27
     Tasks..28
     General Activities.................................57

Wh-Questions
     Contents...59
     Tasks..60
     General Activities.................................89

Grammar
     Contents...93
     Tasks..95
     General Activities................................161

References..163

Answer Key..164

Introduction

This book has been written to help speech-language pathologists, teachers of the learning disabled, parents and other interested individuals in planning remediation activities for clients with auditory or language learning disabilities. This book originated from our frustration in trying to find materials in book or manual form which would provide the quality, variety and range of exercises needed in daily therapy with clients exhibiting varied deficits, abilities, and ages. We were seeking a book which did not require accompanying materials, was not a portion of an expensive kit, and could be used by para-professionals and parents, as well as by speech-language pathologists and teachers.

In presenting this handbook, we have attempted to provide a sufficient amount of material for repeated practice and drillwork, which is vital in the remediation of language deficits. In addition, we have included more difficult exercises to be used with older students and adults. These exercises have also been found to be helpful to post-stroke patients with deficits in auditory processing and verbal expression. All exercises contained within this handbook are or are similar to exercises we generated and implemented daily in our therapy sessions. The various exercises are intended to be used in individual or small group therapy sessions; however, they may also be successfully used in learning centers and self-contained classrooms.

Since *HELP* was first introduced in 1980, we have received overwhelming, enthusiastic response from our colleagues. Our initial goals to produce an inexpensive, practical and quality product apparently were met and appreciated by other professionals, parents and para-professionals in their work with language impaired individuals of all ages. Suggestions for improvement have been noted throughout the years and have been combined with some of our original ideas for the product to bring you the new, improved *HELP* manuals.

Individuals familiar with the original manuals will immediately recognize the new spiral binding designed to give each book greater durability and to aid in photocopying. Limited reproduction of the exercises is now permitted to facilitate the effective use of *HELP* in carryover activities outside the therapy situation. Answers for strictly auditory tasks are printed after the stimuli, as in the original version of *HELP*. The answers for sections to be presented as either visual or auditory tasks have been moved to an answer key section at the back of the manual. This change allows *HELP* to be presented as reading and visual tasks, and not just as auditory tasks.

The IEP goals have been retained and instructions have been added for those individuals utilizing the product in a visual mode. The client experiencing difficulty processing the material either acoustically or visually can benefit from the new format because the auditory + visual mode can more easily be utilized and either the auditory or the visual element can be gradually faded.

HELP is divided into logical chapters covering a broad range of activities. We have included those areas with which we have had the most success, hoping to provide a therapeutic instrument that is economical, practical, and thorough. Activities are provided at the end of each chapter to aid in carryover to everyday situations. The following guidelines are offered for effective utilization of the tasks in *HELP*.

1. Many tasks are presented as written worksheets for the client. Use your own judgment in presenting the tasks orally or as worksheets, depending on the ability of your client and your overall purpose for specific remediation.

2. As the ages and skills of the children or adults will vary, use your own judgment as to which portions of each section should be used for therapeutic sessions. An attempt has been made to rank the exercises, when possible, from the easier items to the more difficult.

3. Common, correct responses have been provided for almost all items in the answer key. There may, however, be other acceptable answers, depending on the client's experiences and cultural background. Again, use your discretion in determining correctness of responses.

4. Many repetitions of items may be necessary before target accuracy levels are reached. Accuracy rates should be kept on the specific items chosen to be within the client's range of ability.

5. Strive to achieve carryover of target concepts in conversation, everyday and classroom activities through constant repetition, questioning and stressing of specific concepts. These exercises may be used by parents and teachers' aides successfully with little explanation from the clinician. Communication between home and school is essential if carryover is to be effective. Auditory processing underlies all language reception, processing, and output. Carryover is essential to derive the maximum benefit from therapy.

The quality, variety and range of materials have not been changed in revising *HELP*. Some adjustments in stimulus items and answers have been made, however, to allow *HELP* to remain current. We hope that the improvements that have been made to the *HELP* manuals will satisfy some, if not all, of the needs expressed to us and to LinguiSystems over the years. Your support and constructive suggestions have been and will continue to be very much appreciated. We hope you will find *HELP* to be beneficial to you in your everyday therapy and instruction experiences.

January 1987   AML
                                                     PMP

Specific Word Finding

Specific word finding tasks are used as a means of building vocabulary and word retrieval skills through association of certain words with common phrases and/or contextual cues. Stimulation of this area through repeated practice of word finding exercises will aid the student in recall of specific words in conversation when common associative cues are present, as well as enhancing speed of recall of common vocabulary words in conversation. Some students may have an adequate receptive knowledge of the vocabulary presented in this section, but need repeated drill work in order to facilitate retrieval of this vocabulary for expressive use.

For some students, it may be helpful or necessary to provide initial phonemic cues for the target words when first working with these exercises. These cues should be gradually faded until word retrieval is accomplished solely with contextual cues.

Task		**Page**
A	Phrase Completion for Initial Verbs	8
B	Phrase Completion for Final Nouns	9
C	Sentence Completion for Final Nouns in Verb Phrases	10
D	Completion of Phrases Containing Prepositions or Conjunctions	12
E	Completion of Final Nouns in Sentences	14
F	Identification of Object Described (Definitions)	17
G	Statement of Items Necessary to Complete Tasks	19
H	Completion of Comparative Phrases	22
I	Completion of Common Sayings and Proverbs	22

Specific Word Finding

Task A: Phrase Completion for Initial Verbs

Fill in the blank to finish each phrase. The first one is done for you.

1. _Open_ the door
2. _____ the light
3. _____ dinner
4. _____ a car
5. _____ a story
6. _____ the television
7. _____ a game
8. _____ a cake
9. _____ the floor
10. _____ a snowman
11. _____ the leaves
12. _____ your hands
13. _____ a book
14. _____ a bow
15. _____ a letter
16. _____ your eyes
17. _____ your shoes
18. _____ the plants
19. _____ a milk shake
20. _____ your hair
21. _____ a ball
22. _____ your feet
23. _____ a kite
24. _____ a fish
25. _____ the phone
26. _____ a bubble
27. _____ an airplane
28. _____ a mountain
29. _____ a fire
30. _____ a knot
31. _____ a movie
32. _____ a bicycle
33. _____ a package
34. _____ the trash
35. _____ the horn
36. _____ a ladder
37. _____ the lawn
38. _____ the steps
39. _____ your belt
40. _____ a balloon
41. _____ a phone call
42. _____ some seeds
43. _____ the window shade
44. _____ a bill
45. _____ a test
46. _____ the salt
47. _____ a match
48. _____ a photograph

49. _____ a question		60. _____ an order	
50. _____ a sweater		61. _____ cement	
51. _____ a walk		62. _____ a toast	
52. _____ the cards		63. _____ a tale	
53. _____ a flat		64. _____ some flour	
54. _____ a race		65. _____ a poem	
55. _____ the leader		66. _____ an answer	
56. _____ the pillow		67. _____ an article	
57. _____ a check		68. _____ a decision	
58. _____ traffic		69. _____ your opinion	
59. _____ a law		70. _____ the issue	

I.E.P. Goal: Given a phrase which is missing an initial verb, the client will complete the phrase with an appropriate verb or verb phrase with 90% or greater accuracy.

Specific Word Finding
Task B: Phrase Completion for Final Nouns

Fill in the blank to finish each phrase. The first one is done for you.

1. A pair of __shoes__
2. A loaf of _____
3. A piece of _____
4. A bottle of _____
5. A glass of _____
6. A drink of _____
7. A bag of _____
8. A pile of _____
9. A spoonful of _____
10. A can of _____
11. A drop of _____
12. A cup of _____
13. A gallon of _____
14. A dish of _____
15. A tube of _____
16. A bunch of _____
17. A carton of _____
18. A pack of _____
19. A pot of _____
20. A bowl of _____
21. A box of _____
22. A load of _____
23. A quart of _____
24. A flake of _____

25. A pound of _____
26. A package of _____
27. A yard of _____
28. A head of _____
29. A swarm of _____
30. A dozen _____
31. A lump of _____
32. A bar of _____
33. A stick of _____
34. A jar of _____
35. A stalk of _____
36. A group of _____
37. A pitcher of _____
38. A cake of _____
39. A bundle of _____

40. A tablespoon of _____
41. A platter of _____
42. A closet of _____
43. A dose of _____
44. A tribe of _____
45. A tin of _____
46. A bushel of _____
47. A bed of _____
48. A peck of _____
49. An ounce of _____
50. A book of _____
51. A packet of _____
52. A flock of _____
53. A side of _____
54. A kilowatt of _____

I.E.P. Goal: Given an incomplete phrase which is missing a final noun, the client will complete the phrase with an appropriate noun with 90% or greater accuracy.

Specific Word Finding
Task C: Sentence Completion for Final Nouns in Verb Phrases

Fill in the blank to finish each sentence. The first one is done for you.

1. We wash our __*hands*__.
2. We play a _____.
3. We read a _____.
4. We kick a _____.
5. We turn on a _____.
6. We sing a _____.
7. We write a _____.
8. We comb our _____.

9. We open the _____.
10. We ride a _____.
11. We draw a _____.
12. We ring a _____.
13. We build a _____.
14. We cut some _____.
15. We drive a _____.
16. We catch a _____.

Copyright © 1987 LinguiSystems, Inc.

17. We climb a _____.
18. We shut the _____.
19. We fly a _____.
20. We color a _____.
21. We hit a _____.
22. We sharpen a _____.
23. We buy some _____.
24. We row a _____.
25. We pick some _____.
26. We button our _____.
27. We curl our _____.
28. We feed the _____.
29. We break a _____.
30. We mow the _____.
31. We paint a _____.
32. We tell a _____.
33. We eat a _____.
34. We jump _____.
35. We listen to a _____.
36. We pound a _____.
37. We dry the _____.
38. We water the _____.
39. We empty the _____.
40. We bend our _____.
41. We stir a _____.
42. We hear a _____.
43. We wipe off the _____.

44. We clean the _____.
45. We do our _____.
46. We scrub the _____.
47. We save _____.
48. We chop some _____.
49. We light a _____.
50. We cash a _____.
51. We saw some _____.
52. We shine our _____.
53. We burn some _____.
54. We iron our _____.
55. We run a _____.
56. We type a _____.
57. We win a _____.
58. We unwrap a _____.
59. We pay a _____.
60. We wind a _____.
61. We milk a _____.
62. We wax a _____.
63. We hang the _____.
64. We mix a _____.
65. We follow _____.
66. We pluck a _____.
67. We shake a _____.
68. We dig a _____.
69. We sift some _____.
70. We decorate a _____.

71. We finish a _____.
72. We bandage a _____.
73. We melt some _____.
74. We lead a _____.
75. We draw the _____.
76. We sand some _____.
77. We pitch a _____.
78. We strum a _____.
79. We repair our _____.
80. We can some _____.
81. We obey the _____.
82. We elect the _____.
83. We press our _____.
84. We strain some _____.
85. We poach some _____.

86. We file some _____.
87. We arrest a _____.
88. We board a _____.
89. We deposit some _____.
90. We witness a _____.
91. We carve a _____.
92. We inflate a _____.
93. We fertilize the _____.
94. We cure a _____.
95. We average some _____.
96. We balance our _____.
97. We tune up a _____.
98. We focus a _____.
99. We ford a _____.
100. We compose a _____.

I.E.P. Goal: Given a sentence with an incomplete verb phrase, the client will complete the sentence with an appropriate noun with 90% or greater accuracy.

Specific Word Finding
Task D: Completion of Phrases Containing Prepositions or Conjunctions

Fill in the blank to finish each phrase. The first one is done for you.

1. peanut butter and _jelly_
2. show and _____
3. Mom and _____
4. soap and _____
5. peek-a- _____
6. pancakes and _____
7. cat and _____
8. brush and _____

9. hug and _____
10. Jack-in-the- _____
11. hot dog and _____
12. queen and _____
13. women and _____
14. salt and _____
15. trick or _____
16. washcloth and _____

17. day and _____
18. ball and _____
19. thunder and _____
20. lettuce and _____
21. wash and _____
22. girls and _____
23. spaghetti and _____
24. tried and _____
25. mop and _____
26. dead and _____
27. robe and _____
28. meat and _____
29. washing machine and _____
30. coast-to- _____
31. forget-me- _____
32. spoon and _____
33. table of _____
34. lock and _____
35. days of the _____
36. sister and _____
37. mother-in- _____
38. scene of the _____
39. peace of _____
40. bow and _____
41. rock and _____
42. The Declaration of _____
43. The Statue of _____

44. justice of the _____
45. breaking and _____
46. stop, look and _____
47. thick and _____
48. hop, skip and _____
49. The Bill of _____
50. now or _____
51. sink or _____
52. hearts and _____
53. give and _____
54. sick and _____
55. chairman of the _____
56. height and _____
57. bait and _____
58. snake in the _____
59. quick and _____
60. lily of the _____
61. cream of the _____
62. pick of the _____
63. plain and _____
64. cream and _____
65. beg, steal or _____
66. fine and _____
67. rough and _____
68. hand in _____
69. hill and _____
70. fun and _____

Copyright © 1987 LinguiSystems, Inc.

71. the chief of _____
72. assault and _____
73. cut and _____
74. freedom of the _____
75. trial and _____
76. bicarbonate of _____
77. right-of- _____
78. attorney at _____
79. brisk and _____
80. hale and _____

I.E.P. Goal: Given an incomplete phrase containing a preposition or conjunction, the client will complete the phrase with an appropriate word with 90% or greater accuracy.

Note: After the client has met target accuracy level for completion of the phrases in this section, he/she should be asked to use each of the phrases in an original sentence, in order to demonstrate understanding of the meaning of the phrases.

Specific Word Finding
Task E: Completion of Final Nouns in Sentences

Fill in the blank to finish each sentence. The first one is done for you.

1. June is my favorite __month__.
2. Would you like a peanut butter and jelly _____?
3. May I have a ~~penny~~ change for the ~~gum~~ washing _____?
4. We bake bread in the _____.
5. Our teacher put our drawings on the bulletin _____.
6. I like to sit in a rocking _____.
7. Val went to the grocery _____.
8. He told us to be ready at eight _____.
9. The chimney is up on the _____.
10. The grass is very dry. We need some _____.
11. Our dog had seven _____.
12. She is a waitress in a _____.
13. He slipped on a banana _____.
14. Do you have change for a _____?
15. The police officer gave Jane a speeding _____.
16. Do you like to ride a Ferris _____?
17. The clerk rang up the sale on the cash _____.

18. Three people were waiting at the bus _____.

19. Turn right at the next traffic _____.

20. Jill is my twin _____.

21. I need to run the vacuum _____.

22. Kate has pierced _____.

23. The frog sat on a lily _____.

24. There is a rip in the shower _____.

25. Pete is a member of his school's marching _____.

26. The movie took place in outer _____.

27. The car stalled on the railroad _____.

28. The dentist put a filling in my _____.

29. I can't see without my _____.

30. For dinner we are having a tossed _____.

31. For snacktime we have some potato _____.

32. While we were driving down the highway, our car had a flat _____.

33. If a boat springs a leak it might _____.

34. Dad told me to stand up _____.

35. We watched them raise the circus _____.

36. Take the kettle off when it starts to _____.

37. Our team has two hits and no _____.

38. We cooked hot dogs on the barbecue _____.

39. When the ambulance approached, we could hear the _____.

40. Seamstresses keep their pins in a pin _____.

41. I need to renew my driver's _____.

42. The mechanic installed a new set of spark _____.

43. I keep my pearls in my jewelry _____.

44. Our new car has front wheel _____.

Copyright © 1987 LinguiSystems, Inc.

45. When dining in a restaurant, one should leave the waiter a _____.

46. We sat on the bleachers on the north side of the football _____.

47. Did you file your income _____?

48. This dress pattern requires a yard of _____.

49. Ed works as a disc jockey at a radio _____.

50. The sign in the theater said "Do not block the _____."

51. Who are you voting for in the next _____?

52. We cooked some chicken in the pressure _____.

53. Put these folders in alphabetical _____.

54. The hockey team scored another _____.

55. Mr. Anderson plays golf at the country _____.

56. The interest rate on our loan is ten _____.

57. To visit Mexico, one must cross the _____.

58. Pioneers moved West in Conestoga _____.

59. Most barns have a hay _____.

60. Italy is a foreign _____.

61. The pharmacist filled the patient's _____.

62. My grandmother keeps her blankets in a cedar _____.

63. The carpenter has a buzz _____.

64. For my birthday I received a box of dusting _____.

65. Genesis is in the Old _____.

66. That rule violates our civil _____.

67. Who is the Chief Justice of the Supreme _____?

68. The judge issued a warrant for his _____.

69. Gold is a precious _____.

70. A moth emerges from a _____.

71. Vermont is one of the states known as New _____.

72. A triangle is a geometric _____.

73. His four of a kind beat my full _____.

74. George passed the test with flying _____.

75. *Ebb* is the word for the falling _____.

I.E.P. Goal: Given a sentence which is missing a final noun, the client will complete the sentence with an appropriate noun with 90% or greater accuracy.

Specific Word Finding
Task F: Identification of Object Described (Definitions)

Write the word in the blank for each definition. The first one is done for you.

1. Babies like to play with these. __toys__
2. It is round and is found on a car. _____
3. People drive these. _____
4. We write on this. _____
5. We sleep in it. _____
6. We turn it on to watch a program. _____
7. It shines in the sky. _____
8. Something that is dialed. _____
9. We use these to cut hair and paper. _____
10. The paper carrier delivers it. _____
11. We use it to wash our hair. _____
12. A baby wears it to keep food off its shirt. _____
13. Where the mail carrier puts the mail when he delivers it. _____
14. Something that opens and shuts and is used to go in and out of rooms. _____
15. It spins around and keeps the air cool. _____
16. We use this to make ourselves clean. _____
17. We open this to let some air into a room. _____
18. The place where food is kept and meals are prepared. _____

Copyright © 1987 LinguiSystems, Inc.

19. Men use these to remove whiskers from their faces. _____

20. Letters are put in these before they are mailed. _____

21. It is found on the end of a pencil and is used when a mistake is made. _____

22. It is attached to a dog's collar when taking it for a walk. _____

23. A shape that has four corners. _____

24. Men keep their money in these and carry them in their pocket. _____

25. It is round and we drink coffee from it. _____

26. People put their cigarette ashes in these. _____

27. It is found in a store. It goes up and down and carries people. _____

28. We take it when we are sick to help us get well. _____

29. Wooden or plastic objects used to hang clothes on the line. _____

30. A game played on a red and black board with squares on it, using red and black, round objects. _____

31. This is poured on a salad to make it tastier. _____

32. Criminals are sent to this place to serve a sentence. _____

33. A type of curl put in a person's hair that lasts a long time and does not wash out. _____

34. A book that tells us what words mean. _____

35. Where a colony of bees lives. _____

36. A body of land surrounded on all sides by water. _____

37. The movable things in a room which are used for sitting on and placing objects on, making it comfortable for living. _____

38. What fire hoses are attached to at the scene of the fire. _____

39. A place where two walls meet at an angle. _____

40. The foam formed by soap and water. _____

41. Cowboys use this for roping animals. _____

42. A group of certain animals, such as sheep or birds. _____

43. A model of the earth showing the oceans and continents. _____

44. The study of the recorded events of the past. _____

45. A book of maps. _____

46. An instrument used for viewing the stars and planets. _____

47. A device used for lifting an automobile a short distance off the ground. _____

48. A child whose mother and father are both dead. _____

49. A pledge in writing that a product will perform satisfactorily for a certain period of time or else it will be replaced. _____

50. A violent storm originating in the tropics, named after a person. _____

51. An official count of the population. _____

52. Slats laid in overlapping rows used to cover roofs and sides of houses. _____

53. A piece of furniture, silverware, etc., made in a former period which has increased in value. _____

54. A Greek-letter organization of men, found on college campuses. _____

55. An official authorized to certify documents and witness signatures. _____

I.E.P. Goal: Given a definition, the client will identify the object described with 90% or greater accuracy.

Specific Word Finding
Task G: Statement of Items Necessary to Complete Tasks

Write what items you need to do each of these things. The first one is done for you.

1. draw a picture __*pencil, paper*__

2. mail a letter _____

3. set the table _____

4. take a bath _____

5. hang a picture on the wall _____

6. build a fire _____

7. make scrambled eggs _____

8. iron a blouse _____
9. light a candle _____
10. bake a cake _____
11. start a car _____
12. make toast _____
13. go fishing _____
14. do the laundry _____
15. build a snowman _____
16. plant a garden _____
17. have a party _____
18. spend the night at your friend's house _____
19. wash your hair _____
20. make a jack-o'-lantern _____
21. trim a Christmas tree _____
22. sew a button on a shirt _____
23. play tennis _____
24. keep dry when it rains _____
25. fix a flat tire _____
26. make a sweater _____
27. go camping _____
28. make a doghouse _____
29. take a picture _____
30. stay afloat in the water _____
31. make a flashlight work _____
32. make a kite _____
33. make a dress _____

34. take your dog for a walk _____
35. get weighed _____
36. decorate Easter eggs _____
37. measure your height _____
38. make jelly _____
39. get stains out of your clothing _____
40. find out how a word is spelled _____
41. make your plants grow better _____
42. thin paint _____
43. put in the collection plate at church _____
44. scuba dive _____
45. fix a leaky faucet _____
46. replace when all the lights in one room go out _____
47. make maple syrup _____
48. find your way on a trip _____
49. be elected to office _____
50. put in the car radiator in the winter _____
51. find the correct direction if you are lost _____
52. relieve a headache _____
53. amplify your voice _____
54. listen to someone's heartbeat _____
55. make a helicoptor fly _____
56. remove a splinter from your foot _____
57. make bread rise _____
58. produce yarn _____
59. obtain before entering a foreign country _____
60. signify the end of a war _____

I.E.P. Goal: *Given a task, the client will name the item(s) necessary for completion of the task with 90% or greater accuracy.*

Specific Word Finding
Task H: Completion of Comparative Phrases

Fill in the blank to complete each phrase. The first one is done for you.

1. As quiet as a __mouse__
2. As busy as a _____
3. As cold as _____
4. As easy as _____
5. As sly as a _____
6. As stubborn as a _____
7. As free as a _____
8. As quick as a _____
9. As clear as _____
10. As tame as a _____
11. As clean as a _____
12. As good as _____
13. As slow as _____
14. As dark as _____
15. As smooth as _____
16. As mad as a _____
17. As skinny as a _____
18. As fit as a _____
19. As hard as a _____
20. As straight as an _____
21. As cool as a _____
22. As old as the _____
23. As pretty as a _____
24. As pleased as _____
25. As high as a _____
26. As gentle as a _____
27. As happy as a _____
28. As hairy as an _____
29. As light as a _____
30. As tough as _____
31. As big as _____
32. As strong as an _____
33. As sharp as a _____
34. As right as _____
35. As fresh as a _____

I.E.P. Goal: The client will complete comparative phrases with an appropriate noun with 90% or greater accuracy.

Specific Word Finding
Task I: Completion of Common Sayings and Proverbs

Complete each sentence with the best word or words. The first one is done for you.

1. Put on a happy __face__.
2. That's the way the _____ crumbles.
3. Don't count your chickens before they _____.

4. You win some and you _____ some.

5. Count your _____.

6. Those were the good old _____.

7. _____ makes perfect.

8. It fits like a _____.

9. There's no fool like an _____.

10. Easy come, easy _____.

11. Fragile, handle with _____.

12. A penny saved is a penny _____.

13. It's like taking _____ from a baby.

14. Like father, like _____.

15. _____ makes waste.

16. The _____ gets the worm.

17. Birds of a feather _____.

18. A stitch in time _____.

19. Look before you _____.

20. The _____ is always greener on the other side.

21. May the _____ win.

22. Make hay while the _____.

23. Too many _____ spoil the broth.

24. _____ is the best teacher.

25. _____ is the best policy.

26. The best things in life are _____.

27. He's burning the _____ at both ends.

28. Thank goodness it's _____.

29. Don't rain on my _____.

30. It's _____ as the crow flies.

31. Out of sight, out of _____.

32. Mark my _____.

33. You can lead a horse to water, but you can't _____.

34. You can't teach an old dog _____.

35. The _____ stops here.

I.E.P. Goal: Given an incomplete saying or proverb, the client will complete the sentence with the appropriate word(s) with 90% or greater accuracy.

Specific Word Finding: General Activities

1. Tell a short story, presenting a picture as key words are spoken. Tell the story again, presenting only the picture in place of the key word and have the student say the word. Tell the story once again, without using the pictures, having the student supply the key words as you pause.

2. Describe an object in the room (by appearance and/or function) or one of a group of pictures placed on the table. Ask the student to guess which item (or picture) you are describing. Then ask the student to describe the picture as you take a turn at recalling the name of the item (or picture) that is being described.

3. Using objects or pictures of objects, ask the student to state actions which can be done with or to the object, stating as many as possible.
   Examples: Think of things that one can do with a spoon.
   (stir with it, wash it, scoop with it, play it, bend it, eat with it, dry it, polish it)
   Think of things that one can do with an envelope.
   (write on it, mail it, seal it, lick it, fold it, rip it, put things in it, put a stamp on it)

4. Using pictures of people or animals, ask the student to state actions which are performed by the person or animal, naming as many as possible.
   Examples: Think of things a father does.
   (works, eats, sleeps, reads, helps, jogs, kisses, plays, yells, drives, understands, coaches)
   Think of things a kitten does.
   (meows, plays, sleeps, eats, chases, purrs, scratches, jumps, drinks milk)

5. Ask the student to keep a list of common phrases or commercial jingles heard on the television or radio during one or two evenings. Then have the students take turns completing the phrases when key words are left out as they are read aloud. Ask the student to make note of common sayings or proverbs they hear others use in conversation, explaining the specific context in which they were used and their meanings.

6. Write definitions on index cards and the corresponding words on separate index cards. After shuffling the two separate decks of cards, ask each student to choose one card from the word pile and one card from the definition pile. Students receive points if they have chosen a matching word and definition or if they are able to trade cards with other students until they have correctly matched the word and definition. This activity could be done with two teams, allowing the students to exchange cards only with other team members.

7. Show the student a picture and ask him to describe it with a comparative statement (as _____ as a _____). For example, when shown a picture of a very old man, the student would be expected to state: "He looks as old as the hills." If

the student exhibits difficulty, make a leading statement (e.g., "He looks old"). If necessary, follow the leading statement with an incomplete sentence: "He looks old. He looks as old as the _____." Students may formulate comparisons which are not commonly used but may still be appropriate (e.g., He looks as old as a century.)

8. Place a collection of objects in a bag or a box. Have the student choose one item. Instruct the student that he is to describe the object without naming the object. He must describe the object using adjectives, adverbs or comparisons to another object. If performed as a classroom activity, the students may keep a list of what they think each student has described, comparing their list to the actual objects after all students have taken their turns. Or this may be done as a team activity, timing how long it takes each team to guess the object described by one of their teammates.

9. Place in a box 15 to 20 slips of paper, each containing a different common verb. The first student is instructed to pick a slip of paper out of the box and then act out the verb listed. The other students are to guess the verb being demonstrated and then insert it in a short phrase or sentence. (Example: *read*—"Read the book" or "Please read the paper.") If there is only one student, the instructor may act out the verbs to be reviewed with the student guessing the answer and providing the appropriate phrase.

10. The student or students are instructed that the words to be guessed all begin with a particular sound (for example, the /b/ sound). The instructor or one of the other students who has been told the mystery word will provide a clue concerning the word, preferably using one-word clues. However, to alter the task, a verb phrase may be used. The other students are to guess the word described. Example: mystery word - *bear;* the students know that the word begins with the /b/ sound. The clue given is "animal"—the students may guess a variety of animals. If they do not think of *bear*, another clue may be given, such as "brown" or "hairy." This activity may be made more interesting by dividing the class into teams with the most points attained by thinking of the appropriate word on the first trial. If the first team misses it on the first trial, the second team has a chance to guess the identity of the mystery word for reduced points. If the second team does not get it, a clue is provided and the first team has another chance with even fewer points awarded if correct. Continue until all words are exhausted. The team with the most points is the winner.

Categorization

Categorization involves both auditory association and specific word finding ability. It is the means by which basic vocabulary is organized and stored for future retrieval. Building of vocabulary skills by association and discrimination of similarities and differences of word concepts provides the organizational ability and semantic groups necessary for verbal expression. It also assists in establishment of an organized base of thoughts and knowledge which is so often lacking among students with auditory learning disabilities.

Task		Page
A	Completion of Categories	28
B	Labeling of Categories	31
C	Discrimination of Categories	35
D	Generation of Categories	39

Categorization
Task A: Completion of Categories

List one or more things that belong to the same category as the words listed. The first one is done for you.

1. apple, cherry, banana, *lime, lemon, strawberry*
2. roast beef, chicken, pork, _____
3. ankle, foot, neck, _____
4. shoe, hat, dress, _____
5. chalk, desk, notebook, _____
6. bird, helicopter, kite, _____
7. ice, snow, Popsicle, _____
8. fire, stove, sun, _____
9. water, juice, milk, _____
10. ball, plate, button, _____
11. cake, pie, pudding, _____
12. cat, dog, skunk, _____
13. seesaw, jacks, slide, _____
14. brick, barbells, bowling ball, _____
15. bed, chair, table, _____
16. candy, potato chips, pretzels, _____
17. hammer, axe, saw, _____
18. fish, coral, seaweed, _____
19. ring, bracelet, locket, _____
20. bat, mitt, mask, _____
21. John, Alex, James, _____
22. Susan, Jennifer, Tammy, _____
23. Smith, Johnson, Myers, _____

24. Texas, Florida, Georgia, _____

25. motorcycle, car, airplane, _____

26. Monday, Friday, Tuesday, _____

27. February, October, June, _____

28. milk, oil, shampoo, _____

29. stethoscope, bandages, medicine, _____

30. banjo, drum, guitar, _____

31. "God Bless America," "Dixie," "Oh Susanna," _____

32. balloon, party hat, cake, _____

33. wasp, ant, bee, _____

34. squash, corn, beets, _____

35. box, bag, jar, _____

36. walnut, cashew, almond, _____

37. diaper, bottles, pins, _____

38. gloves, eyes, shoes, _____

39. gardenia, carnation, lily, _____

40. rain, fog, sleet, _____

41. hat, beret, crown, _____

42. lemon, peach, vanilla, _____

43. Chevrolet, Toyota, Plymouth, _____

44. sparrow, robin, cardinal, _____

45. history, spelling, chemistry, _____

46. aspirin, toothpaste, deodorant, _____

47. Easter, Valentine's Day, Halloween, _____

48. firefighter, lawyer, nurse, _____

49. banana, lemon, corn, _____

50. elastic, stockings, sweater, _____

51. diamond, square, pentagon, _____

52. peanut butter, jelly, egg salad, _____

53. boom, clang, snap, _____

54. skip, run, gallop, _____

55. Earth, Mars, Venus, _____

56. concert, ballet, play, _____

57. Clue, Monopoly, chess, _____

58. poker, hearts, slap jack, _____

59. U.S.A., Italy, Korea, _____

60. Lincoln, Kennedy, Truman, _____

61. sleeping bag, lantern, canteen, _____

62. emerald, ruby, sapphire, _____

63. brother, uncle, grandfather, _____

64. salt, pepper, oregano, _____

65. saw, knife, scissors, _____

66. heart, liver, lungs, _____

67. smell, see, hear, _____

68. badminton, croquet, horseshoes, _____

69. private, corporal, sergeant, _____

70. palm, oak, chestnut, _____

71. Santa Claus, Peter Pan, Easter Bunny, _____

72. corn, rice, oats, _____

73. Yale, Duke, Notre Dame, _____

74. polio, pneumonia, measles, _____

75. *Tom Sawyer, Heidi, Treasure Island,* _____

76. brass, copper, zinc, _____
77. Catholic, Presbyterian, Mormon, _____
78. Edison, Bell, Wright, _____
79. silk, cotton, linen, _____
80. toaster, blender, can opener, _____
81. king, prince, duke, _____
82. rifle, slingshot, cannon, _____
83. Virgo, Libra, Capricorn, _____
84. collie, bulldog, spaniel, _____
85. waltz, polka, tango, _____

I.E.P. Goal: Given three items from a specific category, the client will add one or more items which correctly fit the category with 90% or greater accuracy.

Categorization
Task B: Labeling of Categories

Name the category for each group of words. The first one is done for you.

1. red, blue, green   *colors*
2. b, q, r   _____
3. three, ten, four   _____
4. doll, truck, ball   _____
5. meat, cereal, fruit   _____
6. chair, table, bed   _____
7. dog, fish, cat   _____
8. Sherry, Cindy, Louise   _____
9. Andy, Ted, Michael   _____
10. Spot, Rover, Blackie   _____
11. slipper, boot, sandal   _____
12. swings, seesaw, slide   _____

13. father, sister, mother _____
14. pipe, cigar, cigarette _____
15. moo, chirp, meow _____
16. pencil, pen, crayon _____
17. licorice, taffy, gumdrops _____
18. jack-o'-lantern, witch, ghost _____
19. Hickory Dickory Dock, Humpty Dumpty, Jack and Jill _____
20. blimp, airplane, jet _____
21. merry-go-round, Ferris wheel, roller coaster _____
22. jacket, hat, boots _____
23. dress, slip, earrings _____
24. letter, newspaper, book _____
25. Easter, Halloween, New Year's Day _____
26. doctor, miner, teacher _____
27. taxi, bus, subway _____
28. Cheerios, Special K, Corn Flakes _____
29. ivy, fern, begonia _____
30. baseball, football, hockey _____
31. lamp, lantern, flashlight _____
32. watch, clock, sundial _____
33. puppy, kitten, calf _____
34. ring, plate, bowling ball _____
35. glass, plate, egg _____
36. wallet, bank, coin purse _____
37. rose, lily, orchid _____
38. bell, telephone, chimes _____

39. monkey, tiger, gorilla _____
40. bicycle, roller skates, wagon _____
41. elevator, escalator, stairs _____
42. radio, television, stereo _____
43. silo, barn, chicken coop _____
44. basement, porch, attic _____
45. money, driver's license, charge card _____
46. aspirin, cough syrup, nose drops _____
47. lights, tinsel, balls _____
48. rope, yarn, ribbon _____
49. north, south, east _____
50. paint, oil, alcohol _____
51. parrot, parakeet, dove _____
52. thread, pins, cloth _____
53. fish, crab, octopus _____
54. June, August, December _____
55. barrette, headband, hairpin _____
56. lipstick, eye shadow, rouge _____
57. French, Spanish, Italian _____
58. grass, spinach, peas _____
59. curtains, blinds, drapes _____
60. necklace, necktie, beads _____
61. carpeting, linoleum, rug _____
62. jar, box, bag _____
63. midnight, noon, dawn _____
64. wood, nails, sandpaper _____

65. sheet, blanket, pillowcase _____
66. nurse, doctor, orderly _____
67. perfume, flowers, sachet _____
68. solitaire, bridge, hearts _____
69. furniture polish, cleanser, bleach _____
70. pin, needle, pencil _____
71. violin, viola, harp _____
72. bridle, saddle, reins _____
73. milk, cream, butter _____
74. river, lake, ocean _____
75. button, snap, zipper _____
76. cafeteria, restaurant, dining hall _____
77. mayonnaise, catsup, mustard _____
78. bomb, dynamite, firecracker _____
79. salami, bologna, pastrami _____
80. scale, ruler, yardstick _____
81. knee, ankle, elbow _____
82. no, yes, maybe _____
83. telescope, binoculars, magnifying glass _____
84. linen, denim, nylon _____
85. murderer, robber, arsonist _____
86. Dallas, New York, Miami _____
87. Alabama, Georgia, West Virginia _____
88. rice, wheat, corn _____
89. Pinocchio, Huckleberry Finn, Snow White _____
90. washing machine, clothes dryer, freezer _____

91. blonde, brunette, auburn _____
92. feathers, cotton, leaves _____
93. inch, foot, mile _____
94. secretary, president, treasurer _____
95. Canada, Norway, Israel _____
96. Army, Navy, Air Force _____
97. Cherokee, Seminole, Apache _____
98. tenor, soprano, baritone _____
99. Noah, Moses, Jacob _____
100. Pacific, Indian, Atlantic _____

I.E.P. Goal: Given three items from a category, the client will label the category with 90% or greater accuracy.

Categorization
Task C: Discrimination of Categories

Underline the word that does not belong in each group. Then write the reason it doesn't belong. The first one is done for you.

1. pencil, pen, chalk, <u>door</u> *It's not used for writing.*
2. table, book, newspaper, magazine _____
3. top, doll, green, train _____
4. lion, dog, lamp, cat _____
5. bus, plane, coat, car _____
6. lamb, calf, kitten, dog _____
7. green, pink, salt, navy _____
8. Tuesday, Thursday, birthday, Saturday _____
9. grapefruit, spinach, apple, lime _____
10. hamburger, steak, veal, cheddar _____
11. coffee, soda, crayon, water _____
12. banana, squash, lima beans, peas _____

Copyright © 1987 LinguiSystems, Inc.

13. eleven, thirteen, twenty, date _____
14. brick, ice, snowman, Popsicle _____
15. Jane, Maria, Linda, George _____
16. desk, bowl, table, bed _____
17. elephant, tiger, leopard, dog _____
18. bicycle, scooter, toaster, motorcycle _____
19. thimble, watch, bracelet, necklace _____
20. potato chips, pretzels, pepper, popcorn _____
21. west, east, south, both _____
22. spatula, hammer, wrench, screwdriver _____
23. bat, mitt, glove, sponge _____
24. pie, cole slaw, cake, pudding _____
25. fish, eagle, shark, whale _____
26. shirt, shoe, hat, tablecloth _____
27. oven, toilet, bathtub, sink _____
28. bee, snake, wasp, butterfly _____
29. spelling, gardening, arithmetic, history _____
30. Christmas, Valentine's Day, July Fourth, Saturday _____
31. guitar, piano, valise, violin _____
32. heel, ankle, knee, ear _____
33. towel, sheet, dress, notebook _____
34. ink, perfume, paint, pencil _____
35. cap, beret, crown, belt _____
36. bee, butterfly, hawk, horse _____
37. daisy, tulip, poison ivy, carnation _____
38. preacher, beautician, secretary, child _____

39. cloud, jump, hop, skip _____

40. chain, shoelace, ribbon, yarn _____

41. Cheerios, Rice Krispies, Saltines, Cocoa Puffs _____

42. glass, water, window, mirror _____

43. roller coaster, seesaw, Ferris wheel, tilt-a-whirl _____

44. filing cabinet, typewriter, desk, jukebox _____

45. polish, glue, soap, cleanser _____

46. bib, diaper, blanket, helmet _____

47. cash register, desk, chalk, teacher _____

48. vanilla, strawberry, peach, vinegar _____

49. hopscotch, bingo, astronaut, kickball _____

50. temple, square, circle, triangle _____

51. raft, log, anchor, canoe _____

52. cotton, concrete, feathers, pillow _____

53. corn, banana, egg yolk, grapes _____

54. grass, trees, clouds, television _____

55. radio, television, book, stereo _____

56. June, March, October, Wednesday _____

57. tractor, toaster, blender, coffee pot _____

58. smell, taste, dance, hear _____

59. tent, bathtub, lantern, backpack _____

60. leopard, fox, skunk, snake _____

61. grandmother, neighbor, aunt, uncle _____

62. chicken, cow, horse, zebra _____

63. North Carolina, Utah, Oregon, Chicago _____

64. penny, pea, house, marble _____

Copyright © 1987 LinguiSystems, Inc.

65. mustard, eggs, milk, cheese _____
66. blood, syrup, milk, dirt _____
67. cake, decorations, axe, gifts _____
68. nail, rug, scissors, paper clip _____
69. bag, box, carton, club _____
70. glasses, shoes, magazine, twins _____
71. surfing, skiing, sledding, ice skating _____
72. square, balloon, box, picture frame _____
73. wren, collie, bluejay, sparrow _____
74. oak, pine, palm, hawk _____
75. bus, traffic, cow, taxi _____
76. farmer, silo, haystack, sewer _____
77. tissue, mud, paper, rags _____
78. elastic, pantyhose, sweater, umbrella _____
79. lettuce, eggs, rice, noodles _____
80. bologna, meatloaf, peanut butter, oatmeal _____
81. barber pole, zebra, pig, flag _____
82. passenger car, caboose, engine, galley _____
83. cranberry, pecan, walnut, cashew _____
84. Mars, Earth, Venus, Metro _____
85. funnel, jar, vase, pitcher _____
86. secretary, jockey, treasurer, president _____
87. Star Wars, King Kong, Password, Mary Poppins _____
88. Tango, Baptist, Buddist, Catholic _____
89. mumps, measles, chicken pox, sprain _____
90. individual, club, group, organization _____

91. opera, chorus, choir, jury _____

92. copper, silver, rubber, bronze _____

93. Spain, China, Bolivia, Erie _____

94. president, king, judge, queen _____

95. newspaper, glass, leather, paint _____

96. heart, liver, muscle, brain _____

97. harbor, port, cove, island _____

98. oxygen, mercury, hydrogen, nitrogen _____

99. Andes, Himalayas, Alps, Nile _____

100. Roquefort, Swiss, Parmesan, endive _____

I.E.P. Goal: Given a list of four items, the client will identify which item does not belong in the same category as the other items and give the reason with 90% or greater accuracy.

Categorization
Task D: Generation of Categories

Listen to these category names. Name as many things as you can that go in each category.

1. **Body Parts**
   - ankle
   - arm
   - back
   - chest
   - chin
   - ear
   - elbow
   - eye
   - fingers
   - foot
   - hair
   - hand
   - head
   - knee
   - leg
   - mouth
   - neck
   - nose
   - shoulder
   - stomach
   - toes
   - wrist

2. **Clothing**
   - bathing suit
   - bathrobe
   - belt
   - blouse
   - boot
   - coat
   - dress
   - gloves
   - hat
   - jacket
   - mittens
   - pajamas
   - pants
   - sandals
   - shirt
   - shoe
   - shorts

skirt
slacks
slipper
sock
stockings
sweater
underwear
vest

3. Things Found in a Schoolroom
book
bulletin board
chair
chalk
chalkboard
clock
crayons
desk
eraser
flag
map
notebook
paper
pencil
ruler
students
teacher

4. Things Found in a Grocery Store
aisles
bagboy
bags
bakery goods
candy
canned goods
cashier
cash register
cigarettes
cleaners
dairy products
delicatessen
food
frozen food
grocery carts
magazines
meat
paper goods
pet food
produce
refrigerator
shelves
signs

5. Things That Fly
airplane
balloon
bat
bee
bird
blimp
butterfly
duck
flag
glider
goose
helicopter
kite
ladybug
mosquito
rocket

6. Things That Are Little
ant
BB
bead
bug
button
caterpillar
contact lens
eyelash
grain of rice
grain of sand
keyhole
marble
M & M's
mouse
paper clip
pea
pearl
penny
pierced earring
pin
raisin
seed
snap
thimble
thumbtack

7. Things That Are Big
airplane
auditorium
circus tent
continent
earth
elephant
football stadium
Grand Canyon
mountain
planet
ship
sky
skyscraper
theatre
tree

8. Things That Are Cold
air conditioner
freezer
frost
ice
iceberg
ice cream
ice cube
icicle
milk
North Pole
Popsicle
snow
snowcone

9. Things That Are Hot
boiling water
cigarette
cigarette lighter
cocoa
coffee
fire
hairdryer
heater
light bulb
lighted match
pepper
sauna
soup
stove
summer
sun
toaster

10. Beverages
beer
cider
coffee
Coke
hot chocolate
Kool-Aid
lemonade
milk
orange juice
soda
tea
water
wine

11. Things That Are Round
ball
balloon
bowl
bracelet
bubble
button
circle
clock
coin
cookie
doughnut
hoop
Lifesaver
lollipop
marble
moon
orange
pancake
pea
pearl
plate
ring
saucer
sun
tire
wheel

12. Desserts
banana split
brownie
cake
candy
cobbler
cookies
cupcake

doughnut
éclair
fudge
ice cream
Jell-O
parfait
pie
Popsicle
pudding
sundae

13. Animals
    aardvark
    alligator
    anteater
    armadillo
    baboon
    bear
    beaver
    bird
    boar
    buffalo
    camel
    cat
    chicken
    chipmunk
    cow
    coyote
    deer
    dinosaur
    dog
    duck
    eagle
    eel
    fish
    giraffe
    goat
    goose
    hippopotamus
    horse
    hyena
    jaguar
    kangaroo
    lion
    llama
    mole
    monkey
    moose
    ox
    porcupine
    rabbit

rhinoceros
seal
shark
skunk
snake
tiger
tortoise
turtle
weasel
whale
wolf

14. Farm Animals
    calf
    chicken
    cow
    duck
    goat
    goose
    horse
    lamb
    mule
    pig
    rooster
    sheep

15. Forest Animals
    beaver
    bird
    chipmunk
    deer
    fox
    groundhog
    mouse
    opossum
    owl
    rabbit
    raccoon
    skunk
    snake
    squirrel

16. Zoo Animals
    alligator
    bobcat
    camel
    deer
    elephant
    giraffe
    gorilla

hippopotamus
　　　leopard
　　　lion
　　　monkey
　　　panda bear
　　　polar bear
　　　rhinoceros
　　　seal
　　　sea lion
　　　snake
　　　tiger
　　　toucan
　　　zebra

17. Pets
　　　cat
　　　dog
　　　duck
　　　fish
　　　gerbil
　　　hamster
　　　horse
　　　parakeet
　　　pony
　　　rat
　　　snake
　　　turtle

18. Things Found on a Playground
　　　baseball
　　　football
　　　hopscotch
　　　horseshoes
　　　jacks
　　　jumprope
　　　jungle gym
　　　marbles
　　　merry-go-round
　　　roller skates
　　　seesaw
　　　skateboard
　　　slide
　　　soccer ball
　　　swings
　　　tetherball

19. Things That Are Heavy
　　　airplane
　　　anvil
　　　barbells
　　　boulder
　　　bowling ball
　　　brick
　　　building
　　　cannon
　　　car
　　　chest of drawers
　　　concrete blocks
　　　elephant
　　　house
　　　refrigerator
　　　table
　　　truck
　　　weights

20. Things That Are Light
　　　air
　　　cloud
　　　cotton ball
　　　dandelion
　　　dust
　　　feather
　　　leaf
　　　napkin
　　　Nerf ball
　　　piece of paper
　　　pillow
　　　smoke
　　　sponge
　　　strand of hair

21. Things Found in a Refrigerator
　　　butter
　　　catsup
　　　celery
　　　cheese
　　　eggs
　　　fruit
　　　juice
　　　lettuce
　　　margarine
　　　mayonnaise
　　　meat
　　　milk
　　　mustard
　　　potato salad
　　　salad dressing
　　　yogurt

22. Things Which Are Read
    address book
    almanac
    Bible
    billboard
    book
    catalog
    comic book
    cookbook
    diagram
    diary
    dictionary
    encyclopedia
    form
    greeting card
    instructions
    invitation
    letter
    list
    magazine
    manual
    map
    music
    newspaper
    note
    sign
    telephone book
    will

23. Furniture
    bed
    bookshelf
    chair
    chest
    chest of drawers
    china cabinet
    couch
    crib
    desk
    dresser
    end table
    footstool
    ottoman
    rocking chair
    sofa
    table
    trunk

24. Things That Grow
    beanstalks
    bushes
    children
    flowers
    garden
    grass
    hair
    mold
    nails
    plants
    savings account
    trees
    vines
    weeds

25. Things Found in a Department Store
    cash registers
    clothing
    clothing racks
    dressing rooms
    dishes
    escalators
    jewelry
    mannequins
    mirrors
    pots and pans
    sales clerks
    sheets
    shoes
    towels

26. Snacks
    cake
    candy
    cookies
    fruit
    ice cream
    peanuts
    pizza
    pop
    popcorn
    potato chips
    pretzels
    soda
    sundae

27. Tools
    awl
    axe
    drill
    electric sander
    file
    hammer
    level
    pick axe
    plane
    pliers
    sawhorse
    screwdriver
    shovel
    vise
    wrench

28. Things Found under the Water
    anchor
    buried treasure
    clams
    coral
    eel
    fish
    lobster
    octopus
    oysters
    porpoise
    reef
    rocks
    sandbar
    scuba diver
    seaweed
    shark
    shells
    shipwreck
    sponge
    squid
    submarines
    whale

29. Things That Melt
    butter
    candles
    candy
    chocolate
    crayons
    gold
    ice
    ice cream
    milk shake
    plastic
    popsicle
    snowman
    sugar
    wax

30. Jewelry
    beads
    bracelet
    cufflinks
    earrings
    locket
    necklace
    pearls
    pendent
    pin
    ring
    tie clip
    tie tack
    watch

31. Sports Equipment
    ball
    basketball hoop
    bat
    boxing gloves
    diving board
    fins
    helmet
    lacrosse stick
    mallet
    mask
    mitt
    parachute
    puck
    skis
    snorkel
    tank
    tennis net
    tennis racquet

32. Transportation
    airplane
    bicycle
    boat
    bus
    canoe
    car
    ferry
    helicopter
    horse

hot air balloon
motorcycle
scooter
ship
snowmobile
subway
train
truck
van
wagon

33. Fruit
apple
apricot
banana
blackberry
blueberry
cantaloupe
cherry
grapefruit
grapes
honeydew melon
kumquat
lemon
lime
nectarine
orange
peach
pear
pineapple
plum
raisins
raspberry
strawberry
watermelon

34. Liquids
alcohol
bleach
blood
cough syrup
gasoline
honey
Kool-Aid
mercury
milk
mouthwash
oil
perfume
shampoo
syrup
vinegar
water

35. Things Found in a Doctor's Office
bandages
cotton
examining table
medicine
needle
nurse
pills
scales
stethoscope
thermometer
tongue depressors
waiting room

36. Things to Do on a Vacation
camp
fish
go horseback riding
hike
paint
play games
read
relax
see a movie
shop
sightsee
skate
ski
sleep
sunbathe
swim
take pictures
write postcards

37. Musical Instruments
banjo
bugle
clarinet
cymbals
drum
flute
guitar
harp

harpsichord
harmonica
oboe
organ
piano
saxophone
tambourine
triangle
trombone
trumpet
tuba
viola
violin

38. Things Found at a Party
    balloons
    cake
    candles
    cards
    crepe paper
    decorations
    food
    friends
    games
    gifts
    guests
    hats
    horns
    laughter
    prizes
    soda
    songs
    streamers
    surprises
    treats

39. Insects
    ant
    bee
    beetle
    butterfly
    caterpillar
    cricket
    dragonfly
    firefly
    fly
    grasshopper
    hornet
    katydid
    ladybug
    locust

mosquito
praying mantis
roach
silverfish
spider
termite
tick
wasp

40. Vegetables
    artichoke
    asparagus
    beans
    beet
    broccoli
    brussels sprouts
    cabbage
    cauliflower
    celery
    corn
    cucumber
    lettuce
    okra
    onion
    parsnip
    peas
    potato
    radish
    spinach
    squash
    turnip
    zucchini

41. Things Made of Metal
    bike
    braces
    can
    chain
    coin
    doorknob
    faucet
    file
    hubcap
    nail
    paper clip
    pins
    pipe
    pots and pans
    ring
    staple
    zipper

42. Containers
    bag
    baggie
    basket
    bookbag
    bowl
    box
    bucket
    carton
    crate
    cup
    envelope
    flowerpot
    jar
    package
    pail
    pocket
    purse
    suitcase

43. Things That Float
    boat
    canoe
    cork
    ducks
    inner tube
    leaf
    life preserver
    paper
    plastic bag
    raft
    sponge
    water ski
    wood

44. Things That Sink
    anchor
    brick
    cement block
    chain
    coin
    hammer
    lead
    nail
    paperweight
    rock
    scissors
    ship
    treasure chest

45. Things That Come in Pairs
    bookends
    boots
    earrings
    ears
    eyes
    fins
    glasses
    gloves
    hosiery
    mittens
    pajamas
    pants
    shoes
    shorts
    skates
    skis
    socks
    twins

46. Things That Sparkle
    champagne
    diamonds
    gems
    glass
    glitter
    gold
    jewelry
    star
    sunlight
    tin foil

47. Flowers
    buttercup
    carnation
    chrysanthemum
    crocus
    daffodil
    dahlia
    daisy
    gardenia
    gladiolus
    goldenrod
    iris
    lily
    marigold
    orchid
    petunia
    poppy
    rose

snapdragon
sunflower
tulip
violet
zinnia

48. Things That Are Green
    broccoli
    cabbage
    celery
    cucumber
    emeralds
    grass
    leaves
    lettuce
    limes
    pears
    peas
    plants
    shamrocks
    spinach
    string beans

49. Weather Conditions
    cloudy
    flood
    fog
    frost
    hail
    hurricane
    monsoon
    overcast
    rain
    sleet
    snow
    sunshine
    tornado
    wind

50. Winter Sports
    hockey
    ice fishing
    ice skating
    skiing
    sledding
    snowmobile riding

51. Things Worn on the Head
    beanie
    beret
    bonnet

cap
crown
derby
hat
helmet
sombrero
sweatband
tam
tiara
top hat
turban
veil

52. Ice Cream Flavors
    blueberry
    butter pecan
    butterscotch
    cherry
    chocolate
    chocolate chip
    coconut
    fudge marble
    lemon
    maple nut
    mocha
    peach
    peppermint
    pistachio
    raspberry
    rocky road
    strawberry
    vanilla

53. Names of Cars
    Blazer
    Bronco
    Cadillac
    Chevrolet
    Colt
    Corvette
    Dasher
    Datsun
    Dodge
    Ford
    Maverick
    Monte Carlo
    Monza
    Mustang
    Oldsmobile
    Opel
    Pinto

Plymouth
Rabbit
Rolls Royce
Seville
Skyhawk
Skylark
Sunbird
Toyota
Volkswagen

54. Things That Have Corners
block
book
box
building
cookie sheet
cube
mirror
newspaper
picture frame
room
square
stamp
street
window

55. Birds
bluebird
bluejay
canary
cardinal
crane
crow
dove
eagle
flamingo
hawk
hummingbird
lark
mockingbird
ostrich
owl
parakeet
parrot
peacock
pelican
pigeon
robin
sparrow
wren
whippoorwill
woodpecker

56. Things That Fit in Your Palm
ant
bead
button
contact lens
dime
earring
eraser
jelly bean
key
match
nut
paper clip
pea
pebble
penny
pin
raindrop
ring
tadpole
thumbtack
tooth
vitamin pill
washer

57. Subjects in School
Algebra
Arithmetic
Biology
Calculus
Chemistry
English
Geography
Health
History
Physical Education
Physics
Psychology
Reading
Science
Social Studies
Sociology
Spelling
Typing
Writing

58. Things in a Medicine Cabinet
aspirin
bandages
cotton balls
cough syrup

dental floss
deodorant
eyedrops
hairspray
iodine
laxative
pills
razor
razor blades
shaving cream
thermometer
toothpaste
vaseline
vitamins

59. Things Made of Paper
cards
coloring books
envelopes
facial tissue
gift wrap
kites
lunch bags
magazines
menus
notebooks
programs
reading books
receipts
stationery
straws
tests
tickets
toilet tissue

60. Things Found in the City
banks
billboards
buildings
buses
cars
lights
manholes
museums
offices
parks
pedestrians
police officers
sewers
sidewalks
streets
subways
taxicabs
traffic lights
trains

61. Things Found in the Country
apple cider
barns
beehives
chicken coops
crops
farmers
fields
flowers
gardens
haystack
horses
houses
pasture
pig sty
sheepdog
silos
stables
tractor
wagons

62. Holidays
birthdays
Chanukah or Hanukkah
Christmas
Easter
Father's Day
Halloween
Independence Day
Labor Day
Memorial Day
Mother's Day
New Year's
Passover
St. Patrick's Day
Thanksgiving
Valentine's Day

63. Occupations
artist
butler
carpenter
chef
cook
dancer
dentist

doctor
farmer
firefighter
fisherman
librarian
mail carrier
mechanic
musician
nurse
pilot
police officer
sailor
sales person
secretary
singer
soldier
teacher
truck driver
waiter/waitress

64. Things That Rip
cardboard
checks
cloth
curtains
leaf
notebook
pants
paper
picture
rags
tin foil
tissue

65. Things That are Yellow
banana
butter
buttercup
cheese
chicks
corn
daffodil
dandelion
egg yolk
grapefruit
lemon
sun

66. Things That Stretch
bathing suit
bubble gum

elastic
muscles
pantyhose
rubber
rubber band
silly putty
slingshot
socks
sweater
sweatsuit

67. Shapes
circle
diamond
heart
hexagon
octagon
oval
pentagon
rectangle
semicircle
square
star
triangle

68. Things That Crumble
bread
bricks
buildings
cake
caulking
cement
chalk
cookies
crackers
dirt
dry leaves
plaster of paris
potato chips
rotten wood
sand castle
tombstones

69. Food That Must Be Cooked or Baked Before Eating
beans
bread
cake
coffee
corn

eggs
grits
meat
noodles
oatmeal
pancakes
pie
pizza
popcorn
potatoes
pudding
rice
waffles

70. Food That Can Be Eaten Raw
apples
bean sprouts
berries
cabbage
carrots
cauliflower
celery
grapefruit
lemon
lettuce
lime
mushrooms
nuts
onions
oranges
peaches
pears
pineapple
raisins
spinach
tangerine
tomatoes
watermelon

71. Types of Sandwiches
beef
bologna
cheese
chicken
corned beef
egg salad
ham
jelly
meat loaf
pastrami
peanut butter

pork
reuben
salami
tuna

72. Things That are Striped
awning
barber pole
candy cane
clothing
flag
skunk
tiger
zebra

73. Things Associated with a Train
box car
caboose
coach car
coal car
conductor
dining car
engine
engineer
flat car
freight
locomotive
mail car
passenger
porter
Pullman car
signal tower
ticket
tracks

74. Sounds
bang
bing
boom
clack
clang
click
cling
crackle
crash
ding
dong
fizz
hum
ping
pop

pow
ring
snap
snip
tinkle
whiz

75. Types of Nuts
almond
butternut
cashew
chestnut
filbert
hazelnut
hickory
macadamia
peanut
pecan
walnut

76. Motions/Verbs
crawl
gallop
glide
hop
jog
jump
leap
race
roll
run
skip
slide
spin
step
swing
tiptoe
turn
twist
walk
wiggle

77. Planets
Earth
Jupiter
Mars
Mercury
Neptune
Pluto
Saturn
Uranus
Venus

78. Board Games
Backgammon
Candyland
Checkers
Chess
Chutes and Ladders
Clue
Life
Monopoly
Parchesi
Scrabble
Sorry
Trivial Pursuit
Uncle Wiggily

79. Card Games
Black Jack
Bridge
Canasta
Crazy Eights
Fish
Gin Rummy
Hearts
Old Maids
Pinochle
Poker
Rook
Solitaire
Spades
War

80. Things That Hold Water
bathtub
bucket
canteen
cup
glass
jar
jug
pitcher
plastic bag
pool
sink
vase
water cooler
well

81. Things That Are Transparent
alcohol
floor wax
gasoline

glass
oxygen
plastic
Saran wrap
water
white vinegar
windows

82. Movies
Battle Star Galactica
Benji
Gone With the Wind
Grease
Jungle Book
Lassie
Mary Poppins
Pinocchio
Saturday Night Fever
Snow White
Sound of Music
Star Trek
Star Wars
Superman
The Love Bug
The Pink Panther
The Wizard of Oz

83. Religions
Baptist
Brethren
Buddhism
Catholic
Episcopalian
Greek Orthodox
Judaism
Lutheran
Methodist
Mormon
Moslem
Presbyterian

84. Words That Begin a Question
can
could
how
shall
should
what
when
where
which
who
why
will
won't
would

85. Things That are Opaque
bark
carpeting
fog
ice cream
leather
newspaper
paint
paste
plaster
rubber
wax
wood

86. Favorite Books & Stories
A Christmas Carol
Bible
Cinderella
Gone With The Wind
Heidi
Little Red Riding Hood
Little Women
Nancy Drew
Swiss Family Robinson
The Bobbsey Twins
To Kill a Mockingbird
Tom Sawyer
Treasure Island

87. Countries
Belgium
Canada
China
Egypt
England
France
Germany
India
Italy
Japan
Korea
Mexico
Peru
Soviet Union

Spain
Switzerland
United States

88. Utensils
can opener
corkscrew
dipper
eggbeater
fork
knife
pancake turner
pizza cutter
spatula
spoon
tongs
vegetable peeler
whisk

89. Contagious Diseases
chicken pox
cold
hepatitis
influenza
leprosy
measles
mumps
polio
scarlet fever
smallpox
tuberculosis

90. Metals
brass
bronze
copper
gold
iron
lead
pewter
silver
steel
tin
zinc

I.E.P. Goal: *The client will name one or more members of a category with 90% or greater accuracy.*

Note: This task can be made more difficult by requiring the client to generate an increasing number of items for each category presented or by requiring the client to generate different items for each category presented on successive trials.

Categorization: General Activities

1. Assist the student in generating a notebook or picture book of magazine pictures which are divided in terms of categories. For example, have a section containing fruit items, vegetables, meats, desserts, animals, clothes, transportation items, etc. The student may add items for homework and can use the book to review the material covered in class.

2. Using picture cards, place several cards depicting items belonging to one category on the table. In addition, place one card in a random position with the other cards that is not a member of the first category. Have the student choose the card which does not belong with the others and have him state the reason that item is different.

3. Using picture cards, place several cards of different categories on the table. Give the student a different card and have him choose which of the cards on the table belongs to the same category as the item he is holding in his hand.

4. Bulletin Boards: Have the students generate bulletin boards which classify items into specific, if not opposing, categories. For example, bulletin boards may be created which exhibit only food items or animals, etc. In addition, opposing categories may be displayed on two sides of the board — for example, hot things as opposed to cold things.

5. Magazine Hunt: Give the students magazines containing a variety of pictures. Have them search for items of a given category (e.g., food, furniture, clothing). You can also have a race to see which student can find a category member first.

6. Assign students a category each day for which they must bring pictures of items that belong to that category to be affixed to their notebooks.

7. Classification of objects in a room: Name all of the common categories to be reviewed. Then, ask the student to identify any category he sees and then name an object contained in the category. To expand this activity, have the student visualize a place (e.g., a room at home) and do the same activity as above.

8. Prepare worksheets containing pictures of two or three members each for three categories and randomly mix them on the page. Pointing to one member, have the student identify the category and then circle all other remaining members on the sheet. Continue through the other categories in a similar fashion.

9. Have a race to see how many category names (food, fruits, animals, etc.) the students can think of and list in a 5-10 minute period. Once the race is over and the winner declared, this activity may be expanded by having the students generate as many members of these categories as possible.

10. Category Bingo: Provide each student with a bingo card on which you have listed categorical members. The instructor presents a category name aloud and the student is to place markers on any item on his card that would qualify as a member of that category. The first having a diagonal or horizontal line filled is the winner.

Wh-Questions

This section consists of a variety of questions which incorporate reception, discrimination, association, vocabulary, and memory skills. Answering a specific question involves many language processing skills, and the inability to answer questions can be due to a deficit in one or more of these skill areas.

In order to answer a question, the question must be received by the student, discriminated from other questions, and associated with past experience or knowledge. Specific and appropriate vocabulary must be recalled and the question and answer must be retained for a sufficient amount of time for this assimilation, comparison, and response to occur.

Difficulty is most often encountered in discrimination of the type of question asked. Students may give a *who* response to a *where* question, or tell *how* instead of *why*. For this reason, drill with contrasting *Wh*-Questions is recommended and is included in this section to be used after practice with the various groups of *Wh*-Questions has been done and the various forms have been mastered by the student.

Answering *Wh*-Questions is a fundamental conversational tool and therefore should be incorporated into plans for remediation of expressive language deficits.

Task		**Page**
A	Answering *What*-Questions	60
B	Answering *Who*-Questions	62
C	Answering *Where*-Questions	64
D	Answering *When*-Questions	66
E	Answering *Why*-Questions	68
F	Answering *How*-Questions	70
G	Answering *Which*-Questions	72
H	Answering Situational *What*-Questions	74
I	Answering Contrasting *Wh*-Questions	77
J	Comparison of Objects Using *How*-Questions	82
K	Formulating a *Wh*-Question for a Given Answer	85

Wh-Questions
Task A: Answering *What*-Questions

Answer each question with a word or phrase that makes sense. The first one is done for you.

1. What does a cow give us? _____milk_____
2. What do we bite with? _____
3. What do we do with soap? _____
4. What makes paper stick together? _____
5. What do children do with toys? _____
6. What do people do with books? _____
7. What do we use for eating soup? _____
8. What makes a cake bake? _____
9. What makes the weeds disappear from your garden? _____
10. What makes your clothes clean? _____
11. What makes a kite fly? _____
12. What makes ice melt? _____
13. What are fireplaces made of? _____
14. What do we use a garage for? _____
15. What do dogs do to rabbits? _____
16. What do people do to songs? _____
17. What do mail carriers do with letters? _____
18. What do people do with jewelry? _____
19. What makes a car run? _____
20. What makes a newspaper appear on your doorstep? _____
21. What makes our shoes shine? _____
22. What makes the light come on? _____
23. What makes a bicycle go? _____

24. What makes a plant grow? _____
25. What are bicycles made of? _____
26. What does an airplane look like? _____
27. What does a flower look like? _____
28. What do we say at the end of a prayer? _____
29. What is a trampoline used for? _____
30. What is a thermometer used for? _____
31. What letter comes after *g*? _____
32. What do we put in a glove compartment? _____
33. What do we put on a barbecue grill? _____
34. What does a yellow light mean? _____
35. What does a boomerang do? _____
36. What number is more than a million? _____
37. What does a cow look like? _____
38. What do we put in a canister? _____
39. What time is noon? _____
40. What day comes before Tuesday? _____
41. What is the last month of the year? _____
42. What grows in an orchard? _____
43. What is made when cream is churned? _____
44. What causes blisters? _____
45. What is a bridle used for? _____
46. What language is spoken in Mexico? _____
47. What is an armored truck used for? _____
48. What continent is the USA on? _____
49. What do we baste? _____
50. What type of weather is found in the tropics? _____

I.E.P. Goal: The client will answer What-Questions with 90% or greater accuracy.

Wh-Questions
Task B: Answering *Who*-Questions

Answer each question with a word that makes sense. The first one is done for you.

1. Who likes to play games? _____children_____
2. Who helps people when they are sick? _____
3. Who teaches children to read? _____
4. Who helps people across busy streets? _____
5. Who makes people laugh at the circus? _____
6. Who delivers packages? _____
7. Who writes books? _____
8. Who grows food for people to eat? _____
9. Who is your father's mother? _____
10. Who is your uncle's wife? _____
11. Who fixes pipes? _____
12. Who helps people make long distance phone calls? _____
13. Who paints pictures? _____
14. Who gives a sermon in church? _____
15. Who takes care of children when their parents go out? _____
16. Who picks up the garbage in a truck? _____
17. Who delivers the newspaper? _____
18. Who lives next door? _____
19. Who builds things with wood? _____
20. Who rents apartments to people? _____
21. Who serves food and drinks on an airplane? _____
22. Who drives cars? _____
23. Who is in charge of a school? _____
24. Who leads an Indian tribe? _____

25. Who sells bread, pies and cakes? _____
26. Who flies in a spaceship? _____
27. Who files and types letters? _____
28. Who dances in toe shoes? _____
29. Who digs coal out of a mine? _____
30. Who cleans your school? _____
31. Who repairs electrical wiring? _____
32. Who fixes women's hair? _____
33. Who repairs automobiles? _____
34. Who repairs a washing machine? _____
35. Who cooks food in a restaurant? _____
36. Who marries a bride? _____
37. Who is in charge of the library? _____
38. Who takes your money in a store? _____
39. Who collects the tickets on a train? _____
40. Who cares for sick animals? _____
41. Who takes pictures? _____
42. Who is your aunt and uncle's child? _____
43. Who is in the Army? _____
44. Who makes and repairs shoes? _____
45. Who leads an orchestra? _____
46. Who represents people in court? _____
47. Who repairs watches? _____
48. Who cashes checks in a bank? _____
49. Who designs houses and buildings? _____
50. Who leaves his country to make his home in another one? _____

I.E.P. Goal: The client will answer Who-Questions with 90% or greater accuracy.

Copyright © 1987 LinguiSystems, Inc.

Wh-Questions
Task C: Answering *Where*-Questions

Answer each question with a phrase that makes sense. The first one is done for you.

1. Where do we keep eggs? _in the refrigerator_
2. Where can we find a doctor? _____
3. Where do we go to buy food? _____
4. Where do we go swimming? _____
5. Where do we keep money? _____
6. Where do we find airplanes? _____
7. Where do we buy clothes? _____
8. Where do we keep our clothes? _____
9. Where do we eat our dinner? _____
10. Where do we keep medicine? _____
11. Where do we spend the night if we are on a vacation? _____
12. Where do we look for ants? _____
13. Where do we find sinks? _____
14. Where do we take a car to be repaired? _____
15. Where is a spare tire kept? _____
16. Where do clowns perform? _____
17. Where do squirrels live? _____
18. Where are attics found? _____
19. Where do people go to worship? _____
20. Where do we find typewriters? _____
21. Where does the President live? _____
22. Where do we go to have our shoes fixed? _____
23. Where does a turtle live? _____
24. Where would we find a piano? _____

25. Where do Eskimos live? _____
26. Where are cribs found? _____
27. Where do we go to check out books? _____
28. Where does a person wear a belt? _____
29. Where does a bank keep money at night? _____
30. Where does shrimp come from? _____
31. Where is your heart? _____
32. Where is the Capitol Building? _____
33. Where do we hide things? _____
34. Where is the coldest place in your house? _____
35. Where do we put newspapers when we have finished reading them? _____
36. Where are paintings displayed? _____
37. Where do we find satellites? _____
38. Where does lumber come from? _____
39. Where do bats live? _____
40. Where do race horses live? _____
41. Where does coal come from? _____
42. Where do subways run? _____
43. Where is the Statue of Liberty? _____
44. Where is Japan? _____
45. Where is Paris? _____
46. Where are glaciers found? _____
47. Where is the equator? _____
48. Where is milk pasteurized? _____
49. Where does a chemist work? _____
50. Where does an orchestra sit offstage? _____

I.E.P. Goal: The client will answer Where-Questions with 90% or greater accuracy.

Wh-Questions
Task D: Answering *When*-Questions

Answer each question with a word or phrase that makes sense. The first one is done for you.

1. When do we take a bath? _when we are dirty_
2. When do we wake up? _____
3. When do we go to school? _____
4. When do we eat cereal? _____
5. When is the news on TV? _____
6. When do we put a new tire on our car? _____
7. When do we wear a coat? _____
8. When do we clap at a show? _____
9. When do we hold our breath? _____
10. When is your birthday? _____
11. When do we cross the street? _____
12. When do we have dessert? _____
13. When do we turn on the air conditioner? _____
14. When do we hang up stockings on the mantel? _____
15. When do we go to the emergency room? _____
16. When do we put new batteries in a flashlight? _____
17. When do we close our eyes? _____
18. When do we brush our teeth? _____
19. When do we pack a suitcase? _____
20. When do we sleep? _____
21. When do we turn the lights out? _____
22. When do we fill up the gas tank? _____
23. When do buds appear on the trees? _____
24. When do we go swimming? _____

25. When do we open the door? _____
26. When do we buy new shoes? _____
27. When do we eat dinner? _____
28. When do we return our library books? _____
29. When do the leaves fall off the trees? _____
30. When is Valentine's Day? _____
31. When do we wear green? _____
32. When does the sun set? _____
33. When is Halloween? _____
34. When is spring? _____
35. When is a tomato ready to eat? _____
36. When is harvest time? _____
37. When does frost appear on the window? _____
38. When does the sun rise? _____
39. When is Independence Day? _____
40. When is school over? _____
41. When is Thanksgiving? _____
42. When is New Year's Eve? _____
43. When is Labor Day? _____
44. When do we have an intermission? _____
45. When was America discovered? _____
46. When is a football game over? _____
47. When do we walk on tiptoes? _____
48. When was the *Declaration of Independence* written? _____
49. When are taps played? _____
50. When do we make resolutions? _____

I.E.P. Goal: The client will answer When-Questions with 90% or greater accuracy.

*Wh-*Questions
Task E: Answering *Why-*Questions

Answer each questions with a phrase that makes sense. The first one is done for you.

1. Why do people wear coats in the winter? _to keep them warm_
2. Why does a man go to the barber shop? _____
3. Why do we brush our hair? _____
4. Why do we go to the bakery? _____
5. Why do cars have lights? _____
6. Why do we wear gloves? _____
7. Why is it easier to ride a bicycle than a unicycle? _____
8. Why do people wear shoes? _____
9. Why don't we walk in the street? _____
10. Why don't we put ice cream in the oven? _____
11. Why do we go to school? _____
12. Why do we eat dinner? _____
13. Why do children do their homework? _____
14. Why do houses have doors? _____
15. Why do stairs have railings? _____
16. Why do we pick up the phone? _____
17. Why do we wear a raincoat? _____
18. Why do pants have pockets? _____
19. Why do we close the windows in winter? _____
20. Why do lights have switches? _____
21. Why do we need a potholder? _____
22. Why do shirts have buttonholes? _____
23. Why do we smile? _____

24. Why do we drink water? _____

25. Why do bathtubs have drains? _____

26. Why do dogs bark? _____

27. Why do we put our socks on before our shoes? _____

28. Why do people have teeth? _____

29. Why do we wear seat belts in the car? _____

30. Why are there lines painted on the road? _____

31. Why do babies sleep in cribs? _____

32. Why do houses have windows? _____

33. Why don't socks have buttons? _____

34. Why do trains have whistles? _____

35. Why do watches have hands? _____

36. Why don't boats have wheels? _____

37. Why do leaves fall off the trees in autumn? _____

38. Why do people have eyelids? _____

39. Why do scissors have two handles? _____

40. Why don't skates have square wheels? _____

41. Why do pencils have erasers? _____

42. Why do records have holes in the middle? _____

43. Why do we put a stamp on a letter? _____

44. Why do we step over puddles when it rains? _____

45. Why do we hold our breath when we dive in the water? _____

46. Why do we turn off the oven when we are through cooking? _____

47. Why do we stop the car at a stop sign? _____

48. Why do we turn off the light when we go to bed? _____

49. Why do we cut the grass? _____

50. Why do we put mayonnaise in the refrigerator? _____

I.E.P. Goal: *The client will answer Why-Questions with 90% or greater accuracy.*

Wh-Questions
Task F: Answering *How*-Questions

Answer each question with a word or phrase that makes sense. The first one is done for you.

1. How does a turtle move? _____*slowly*_____

2. How do we act when someone is asleep? _____

3. How do we dry clothes? _____

4. How do we make a bike go? _____

5. How do we know if it is going to rain? _____

6. How do we know if something is on fire? _____

7. How do we know if we have a flat tire? _____

8. How do we know if the sidewalk is slippery? _____

9. How do we know if there is a crack in our glass? _____

10. How do we know if there is a nail in our shoe? _____

11. How do we know when to get up in the morning? _____

12. How do we know when to buy new socks? _____

13. How do we make toast? _____

14. How do we know if we received any mail? _____

15. How do we know if something is sweet? _____

16. How do we know if someone is knocking on the door? _____

17. How do we know when to change a light bulb? _____

18. How do we know if the floor needs scrubbing? _____

19. How do we know when to go to the grocery store? _____

20. How do we know _____
21. How do we know when a movie is over? _____
22. How do we know if the refrigerator isn't working? _____
23. How do we know if our scissors need sharpening? _____
24. How do we know if we have the wrong house key? _____
25. How do we know if a car has driven through our yard? _____
26. How do we know if someone has used our towel? _____
27. How do we know if a letter was put in our mailbox by mistake? _____
28. How do we know what someone's telephone number is? _____
29. How do we know what time a certain television show begins? _____
30. How do we know what size sweater our father wears? _____
31. How do we know what city we were born in? _____
32. How do animals keep warm in the winter? _____
33. How do we know when school is closed because of snow? _____
34. How do we know what day of the week our birthday is on? _____
35. How do we know when summer is over? _____
36. How do we know when school is over for the day? _____
37. How do we know when a store is open? _____
38. How do we know when the car is out of gas? _____
39. How do we know if something is rough? _____

40. How do we know how many eggs to put in a cake? _____

41. How do we know what size shoes we wear? _____

42. How do we get somewhere if we don't have a car? _____

43. How do we remember which page we were on when we stopped reading a book? _____

44. How do we know if something has faded in the washing machine? _____

45. How do we know which state is next to ours? _____

46. How do we know if we have gained weight? _____

47. How do we know if a street is one-way? _____

48. How do we get a driver's license? _____

49. How do we hold bricks together? _____

50. How does a pilot land a plane in the dark? _____

I.E.P. Goal: The client will answer How-Questions with 90% or greater accuracy.

Wh-Questions
Task G: Answering Which-Questions

Circle the word that is the best answer for each question. The first one is done for you.

1.	Which is worn on the wrist?	(bracelet)	ring
2.	Which would you rather do on a vacation?	go to the beach	go to the hospital
3.	Which do you attend on Sunday morning?	school	church
4.	Which would you find in a space ship?	astronaut	skater
5.	Which goes under the ground?	bridge	tunnel
6.	Which would you rather ride on?	bicycle	turtle
7.	Which do we put on cereal?	milk	mayonnaise
8.	Which would you rather have for a pet?	leopard	rabbit
9.	Which would you find on the beach?	driftwood	roses
10.	Which of these is used when painting a room?	roller	easel

11.	Which corner of an envelope do you put a stamp on?	top	bottom
12.	Which goes under the water?	ocean liner	submarine
13.	Which is not a weapon?	bow and arrow	hairbrush
14.	Which will bend before it will break?	pretzel	a straw
15.	Which color is found on the United States flag?	red	green
16.	Which is part of a car engine?	blender	carburetor
17.	Which color means *stop?*	red	green
18.	Which is not found in a library?	book	wrench
19.	Which would hold water?	basket	pitcher
20.	Which is easier to fix?	broken watch	torn pants
21.	Which can be bought in a dime store?	watermelon	stapler
22.	Which color is cooler to wear?	white	black
23.	Which side of the road do we drive on?	left	right
24.	Which would a child play with?	a saw	a game
25.	Which is a vegetable?	celery	pear
26.	Which would you see in a school room?	carousel	desk
27.	Which would not be deep?	ocean	bathtub
28.	Which item is used when hiking?	high heels	backpack
29.	Which would not be found at a swimming pool?	surf	a lifeguard
30.	Which is horizontal?	door	floor
31.	Which should not be left within reach of small children?	jelly	bleach
32.	Which dissolves in hot water?	instant coffee	rice
33.	Which is found in a Christmas stocking?	candy	kite
34.	Which is sold only in pairs?	shoe	jacket
35.	Which animal would a bird fear more?	cat	squirrel

36.	Which is not the name of a color?	pickle	aqua
37.	Which one is the name of a hair color?	chrome	blonde
38.	Which one is found in a book?	chapter	a temple
39.	Which one is the name of a candy flavor?	licorice	tenement
40.	Which one would fit inside a wedding ring?	raisin	plum
41.	Which one would an Indian have?	carousel	tomahawk
42.	Which is woven?	cloth	countertop
43.	Which can hold more liquid?	a quart jar	a gallon jug
44.	Which follows an orbit?	TV	planet
45.	Which needs constant attention?	plant	baby
46.	Which country is in Europe?	Japan	France
47.	Which animal is a mammal?	snake	cow
48.	Which is not a former president?	Ben Franklin	Abe Lincoln
49.	Which has more angles?	triangle	square
50.	Which cannot be traced?	phone call	shoe

I.E.P. Goal: The client will answer Which-Questions with 90% or greater accuracy.

*Wh-*Questions
Task H: Answering Situational *What-*Questions

Answer each question to explain what you would do. The first one is done for you.

1. What would you do if you spilled your milk?   *clean it up*

2. What would you do if you went to the grocery store and forgot your money? _____

3. What would you do if your newspaper was left out in the rain? _____

4. What would you do if it started to rain on a picnic? _____

5. What would you do if you had a headache? _____

6. What would you do if you hit a baseball through your neighbor's window? _____

7. What would you do if you bought a sweater for your mother and it was the wrong size? _____

8. What would you do if you stepped on a nail? _____

9. What would you do if you had a toothache? _____

10. What would you do if you dropped a glass? _____

11. What would you do if your television broke? _____

12. What would you do if you ripped your sleeve? _____

13. What would you do if you lost your jacket? _____

14. What would you do if you got locked in a bathroom? _____

15. What would you do if you left the freezer door open? _____

16. What would you do if you were invited to two parties at the same time? _____

17. What would you do if your bicycle had a flat tire? _____

18. What would you do if a storm knocked down a power line in your yard? _____

19. What would you do if you forgot your friend's birthday? _____

20. What would you do if you sat in wet paint? _____

21. What would you do if you dialed the wrong number? _____

22. What would you do if you lost your house key? _____

23. What would you do if your car got stuck in the snow? _____

24. What would you do if you burned the dinner? _____

25. What would you do if you were late to school? _____

26. What would you do if you were swimming and it started to lightning? _____

27. What would you do if a stranger offered you a ride? _____

28. What would you do if you dropped your sandwich on the ground? _____

29. What would you do if you broke your friend's new watch? _____

30. What would you do if your kite got caught in a tree? _____

31. What would you do if you went on a trip and forgot your toothbrush? _____

32. What would you do if you dropped your tray in the cafeteria? _____

33. What would you do if you got chewing gum in your hair? _____

34. What would you do if you saw two children fighting on the playground? _____

35. What would you do if the phone rang and you were in the bathtub? _____

36. What would you do if you got a splinter in your finger? _____

37. What would you do if bugs were eating the vegetables in your garden? _____

38. What would you do if you only had two cupcakes for four people? _____

39. What would you do if your book was overdue at the library and you could not find it? _____

40. What would you do if it was a very cold night and the furnace stopped working? _____

41. What would you do if your car broke down on a deserted road? _____

42. What would you do if you needed an ambulance and didn't have a telephone book? _____

43. What would you do if a clerk gave you the wrong change? _____

44. What would you do if you saw a holdup through the bank window? _____

45. What would you do if you got off at the wrong bus stop? _____

46. What would you do if your faucet sprang a leak? _____

47. What would you do if you left your crayons in the sun and they melted? _____

48. What would you do if you got lost in the woods? _____

49. What would you do if someone began telling you a joke you already knew? _____

50. What would you do if you walked on the kitchen floor while your mother was waxing it? _____

I.E.P. Goal: The client will answer situational What-Questions with 90% or greater accuracy.

Wh-Questions
Task I: Answering Contrasting Wh-Questions

Answer each set of questions with phrases that make sense. The first set is done for you.

1. Where do we sleep? *in bed*

   When do we sleep? *at night*

   Why do we sleep? *because we are tired*

2. When do we eat? _____

   Where do we eat? _____

   What do we eat? _____

3. Where do we wash our clothes? _____

   When do we wash our clothes? _____

   What do we use to wash our clothes? _____

4. When do we take a bath? _____

   Why do we take a bath? _____

   Where do we take a bath? _____

5. Where do we watch television? _____

   When do we watch television? _____

   Why do we watch television? _____

6. Why do we use a lawn mower? _____

   When do we use a lawn mower? _____

   Where do we keep a lawn mower? _____

7. Who rides a bicycle? _____

   Why do we ride a bicycle? _____

   Where do we ride a bicycle? _____

8. Where do we find an escalator? _____

   When do we ride an escalator? _____

   Why do we have escalators? _____

9. Who uses a thermometer? _____

   Why do we use thermometers? _____

   Where do we keep a thermometer? _____

10. When do we plant flower seeds?

    Where do we plant flower seeds?

    Why do we plant flower seeds?

11. Who uses a saw?

    When do we use a saw?

    Where do we buy a saw?

12. Where do we find a mailbox?

    What do we use a mailbox for?

    Who delivers our mail?

13. Why do we use a ladder?

    Who uses a ladder?

    When do we use ladders?

14. Where do we find a chimney?

    When do we need a chimney?

    Why do we need a chimney?

15. Where do you go to school?

    Why do you go to school?

    When do you go to school?

16. Where do we find mirrors?

    Why do we have mirrors?

    When do we use a mirror?

17. Who uses a garden hose? _____

    Why do we have garden hoses? _____

    When do we use a garden hose? _____

18. When do we fly a kite? _____

    Who likes to fly kites? _____

    Where do we fly kites? _____

19. Why do we use a mop? _____

    Where do we use a mop? _____

    What do we do with a mop? _____

20. Where do we go ice skating? _____

    When do we go ice skating? _____

    What do we use to go ice skating? _____

21. Why do we use a teakettle? _____

    Where do we use a teakettle? _____

    What do we put in a teakettle? _____

22. Who uses a slide? _____

    Where do we find slides? _____

    Why do we like slides? _____

23. What is a tow truck used for? _____

    When do we call a tow truck? _____

    Where do we get a tow truck? _____

24. What is a hammer used for? _____

    Who uses a hammer? _____

    Where do we keep hammers? _____

25. Why do we use rulers? _____

    When do we use rulers? _____

    What is a ruler made of? _____

26. Where do we use snow skis? _____

    Why do we use snow skis? _____

    What type of store would sell snow skies? _____

27. When do we need sunglasses? _____

    Why do we wear sunglasses? _____

    Where do we wear sunglasses? _____

28. Where are refrigerators found? _____

    Why do we have refrigerators? _____

    What is kept in a refrigerator? _____

29. Why do we ride horses? _____

    Who rides a horse in a race? _____

    Where is a horse kept? _____

30. What do we do with a sieve? _____

    Where would we find a sieve? _____

    Who would use a sieve? _____

31. Where is a jury found? _____

    Who is on a jury? _____

    Why do we have a jury? _____

32. Where do we go to get a manicure? _____

    When do we get a manicure? _____

    Who gives a manicure? _____

33. Where do we find odometers? _____

    What does an odometer measure? _____

    When do we use an odometer? _____

34. What is a mill used for? _____

    Who uses a mill? _____

    What product is made at a mill? _____

35. Where would an exhibit be found? _____

    What would be found in an exhibit? _____

    Whose work would be found in an exhibit? _____

I.E.P. Goal: The client will answer contrasting Wh-Questions with the same referent with 90% or greater accuracy.

Wh-Questions
Task J: Comparison of Objects Using *How*-Questions

Give one difference between the objects in each question. The first one is done for you.

1. How is paste different from glue? *It is not a liquid.*

2. How is a cake different from a pie? _____

3. How is a banjo different from a guitar? _____

4. How is a shirt different from a jacket? _____

5. How is a boot different from a shoe? _____

6. How are toenails different from fingernails? _____

7. How is a ring different from a bracelet? _____
8. How is a motorcycle different from a bicycle? _____
9. How is a blanket different from a sheet? _____
10. How is a needle different from a straight pin? _____
11. How is a couch different from a bed? _____
12. How is hair different from a wig? _____
13. How is a brush different from a comb? _____
14. How is a dresser different from a desk? _____
15. How is a water ski different from a snowshoe? _____
16. How is an apartment different from a house? _____
17. How is Jell-O different from pudding? _____
18. How is a pair of sandals different from a pair of loafers? _____
19. How is a penny different from a dime? _____
20. How is a chicken different from a duck? _____
21. How is a saucer different from a plate? _____
22. How is a broom different from a mop? _____
23. How is perfume different from after-shave lotion? _____
24. How is a bridge different from a tunnel? _____
25. How is a match different from a cigarette lighter? _____
26. How is a road different from an alley? _____
27. How is soccer different from football? _____
28. How is a horse different from a camel? _____
29. How are contact lenses different from glasses? _____
30. How is a paper clip different from a staple? _____
31. How is margarine different from butter? _____

Copyright © 1987 LinguiSystems, Inc.

32. How is a flower different from a weed?

33. How is a raisin different from a grape?

34. How is a tiger different from a leopard?

35. How is sleet different from rain?

36. How is a notebook different from a tablet?

37. How is a pair of pliers different from a wrench?

38. How is a life preserver different from an inner tube?

39. How is a fishing lure different from bait?

40. How is an alligator different from a crocodile?

41. How is a violin different from a viola?

42. How is a map different from a globe?

43. How is a play different from a novel?

44. How is a dictionary different from an encyclopedia?

45. How is a cast different from a splint?

46. How is a compass different from a weather vane?

47. How is a fender different from a bumper?

48. How is a hoe different from a shovel?

49. How is a hotel different from a motel?

50. How is a minister different from a rabbi?

51. How is an essay different from a short story?

52. How is a pickle different from a cucumber?

53. How is an allowance different from a salary?

54. How is a balcony different from a porch?

55. How is biology different from history?

56. How is plaster different from cement?

57. How is a funnel different from a strainer? _____

58. How is a suggestion different from an order? _____

59. How is a monument different from an statue? _____

60. How is a vein different from an artery? _____

I.E.P. Goal: The client will recognize differences between two objects when asked How-Questions with 90% or greater accuracy.

Note: The above items may be repeated in reverse order for further practice on this skill. For example, item 1 would read: How is glue different from paste?

Wh-Questions
Task K: Formulating a Wh-Question for a Given Answer

I. Write a question starting with *What* for each answer. The first one is done for you.

1. a hat *What do we wear on our heads?*

2. a song _____

3. toothpaste _____

4. a bird _____

5. nine o'clock _____

6. four _____

7. December _____

8. mustard _____

9. snow tires _____

10. a noise _____

II. Write a question starting with *Who* for each answer. The first one is done for you.

1. Santa Claus *Who brings toys at Christmas?*

2. a pilot _____

3. a student _____

4. a mother _____

5. a lifeguard _____

6. a passenger _____

7. an usher _____

8. a hostess _____

9. an athlete _____

10. the governor _____

III. Write a question starting with *Where* for each answer. The first one is done for you.

1. in a house *Where do people live?*

2. in the refrigerator _____

3. on our wrist _____

4. next door _____

5. on the table _____

6. in our wallet _____

7. in the oven _____

8. in the bathtub _____

9. to the drycleaners _____

10. at school _____

IV. Write a question starting with *When* for each answer. The first one is done for you.

1. twelve o'clock *When is midnight?*

2. on Saturday _____

3. June, July, August _____

4. at night _____

5. when it is cold outside _____

6. when we are tired _____

7. when it is done _____

8. at dawn _____

9. April 1 _____

10. never _____

V. Write a question starting with *Why* for each answer. The first one is done for you.

1. because it is raining outside __Why do we take an umbrella?__
2. because it is dark _____
3. because it is too heavy _____
4. because they do not have wings _____
5. so it will not melt _____
6. so they can see better _____
7. to find out what time it is _____
8. because it might break _____
9. so it will write better _____
10. to protect their heads _____

VI. Write a question starting with a *Wh*-Question word that makes sense with the answer. The first one is done for you.

1. three o'clock __What time is school over?__
2. because it is hot outside _____
3. a book _____
4. in the closet _____
5. water _____
6. an umpire _____
7. Saturday and Sunday _____
8. a baby _____
9. in the ocean _____
10. in case we have a flat tire _____
11. a prison _____
12. pick it _____
13. at a dock _____
14. when we are unhappy _____

Copyright © 1987 LinguiSystems, Inc.

15. because they might get cut _____
16. a king _____
17. Superman _____
18. a mink _____
19. Cinderella _____
20. because it is too expensive _____
21. purple _____
22. when we are camping _____
23. because it squeaks _____
24. Christopher Columbus _____
25. an eagle _____
26. at a pharmacy _____
27. on the desert _____
28. Betsy Ross _____
29. tobacco _____
30. Thomas Edison _____
31. so they do not wilt _____
32. to change the order in which they are dealt _____
33. a thermos _____
34. in a convent _____
35. in a belfry _____
36. daily _____
37. a dam _____
38. at an observatory _____
39. during a depression _____
40. a skeleton _____

I.E.P. Goal: The client will ask appropriate Wh-Questions when presented with a variety of answers.

Wh-Questions: General Activities

1. Have the student make a *Wh*-Question notebook using pictures cut from magazines. Label each page for the categories *who, what, when* and *where,* and have the student find and cut out pictures which answer each of these questions. For example, a picture of a boy would be pasted on the *who* page, a picture of a shoe on the *what* page, a picture of a house on the *where* page and a picture of Christmas time on the *when* page. Then go through the notebook with the student, asking him *Wh*-Questions for each picture in the notebook. Then ask the student to go through the notebook, asking *Wh*-Questions for each picture in the notebook.

2. Paste pictures depicting answers to various *Wh*-Questions on index cards. Place two, three or four cards on the table, asking a *Wh*-Question and instructing the student to choose the correct picture to answer the question as he also states the answer aloud. Then have the student take a turn asking the questions, as the clinician gives the appropriate answer in sentence form.

3. Using a picture which depicts a scene (such as a man outside watering the lawn), ask the student contrasting *Wh*-Questions regarding the scene (e.g., Who is outside?, Where is the man?, What is the man carrying?, Why is the man outside?). If the student gives inappropriate answers, cue him by pointing to the appropriate portion of the picture. Initially the student may respond with single words or phrases, but eventually he should be required to respond in full sentences.

4. Introduce community helpers by using pictures, stories, filmstrips and/or visitors to the classroom and field trips. After all community helpers have been studied, place their pictures on the table, asking *Who*-Questions (e.g., Who delivers the mail?, Who helps us when we are sick?, etc.), having the student choose the correct picture as he answers the question. Then ask *What*-Questions for objects associated with community helpers by use (e.g., What does a firefighter ride in?) and for functions performed by community helpers (e.g., What does a pharmacist do?).

5. Read sentences of the form: noun + is + verb + ing + object to the student. Ask *Wh*-Questions following each sentence.
   For example: Lucy is wearing the yellow dress.
             Who is the girl? Lucy
             What is she wearing? a yellow dress

   Read sentences of the form: noun + verb(s) + object + modifier to the student. Ask *Wh*-Questions following each sentence.
   For example: Students ride school buses to the football game.
             Where are they going? to the football game
             What do they ride? school buses
             Who rides the buses? students

   Continue as noted above for sentences of increasing length and complexity.

6. Instruct the student that you are going to state answers to various questions (who, what, when, where, how, why) and they are to state what type of question was asked.
   For example: boat (*What*-Question)
                   on the table (*Where*-Question)
                   Mrs. Temple (*Who*-Question)
                   November 1 (*When*-Question)
                   slowly (*How*-Question)
                   because it is raining (*Why*-Question)

   Then reverse the activity, instructing the student to state an answer that would be given to a specific type of question.
   For example: give an answer for a *Who*-Question (Aunt Sally)
                   give an answer for a *When*-Question (yesterday)
                   give an answer for a *How*-Question (by looking outside)
                   give an answer for a *Where*-Question (downstairs)
                   give an answer for a *What*-Question (ink)
                   give an answer for a *Why*-Question (because it is dangerous)

   The goal of these activities is to help the student acquire knowledge of categories of questions and answers. Although the ability to answer a specific question is not necessary for this activity, it may be expanded to include this task. For example, after the student has stated the type of question asked, he may then be asked to formulate an appropriate question for the answer given, as in the exercises in the chapter.

7. Choose a number of places located in the classroom which will be used for placement of previously selected objects. The student should remember the various places or can be given a list of the places if unable to remember them. When the student is out of the room, place the various objects around the room in the predetermined locations. The student is then asked to return to the room with his back to the locations of the objects. The student may then ask a certain number of *What*- or *Where*-Questions in order to determine the location of a specific object. The student may not, however, use the name of the object he is seeking in any question. Questions which may be used would include: Where is the pencil?, What is on the teacher's desk?, What is one object that is not on the bookshelf? By a process of elimination and reasoning, the student should be able to locate the object by asking a certain number of questions. It should be determined before beginning the activity how many questions the student is allowed to ask and the student should not be allowed to ask as many questions as there are locations. This will prevent the student from asking "What is on the _____?" for each location until he finds the object. The student should be allowed to write down information as it is acquired, and a list of objects may be supplied prior to beginning the questions. If enough locations are available in which the object can be hidden out of sight, the student need not keep his back to the room when asking the questions; this may provide him visual cues in formulating his questions.

8. Present the student with a list of items (e.g., shampoo, bread, tires, stockings). Have him state where he would go to purchase each item. Then ask *Where*-Questions in random order from the original list.

9. Give the student a list of chores to do or information to obtain (e.g., getting shoes repaired, getting the car inspected, having your teeth cleaned, getting a passport). Have the student state where he would go to accomplish each task. Then ask *Where*-Questions in random order from the original list.

10. Give the student a list of household objects (e.g., pot holders, bureau, pliers, furnace). Have him state where he would go to find each object in his house. Then ask *Where*-Questions in random order from the original list.

11. Tell the student that he is going to a particular place (e.g., to the beach, camping, shopping, skiing). Have him state items necessary for each activity — items one should take when going to these particular places. Then ask *Where*-Questions from his list of answers (e.g., Where are you going if you are taking your bathing suit?, etc.)

12. Combine all *Where*-Questions from the previous four exercises in random order.

13. For practice in answering situational *What*-Questions, have the student take turns as the writer of an advice column. Other students in the class would be instructed to formulate situations (e.g., "Every morning when I walk to the bus stop, a dog chases me." "I borrowed my mother's purse without asking her and got ink on it."). The student who is posing as the writer of the advice column would be asked to answer the students' letters (can be done aloud) with an appropriate solution to the situation. All letters should include a statement of the problem in the form of a *What*-Question (e.g., What would you do if...?). Students should take turns asking and answering the questions.

Grammar

Grammar represents the individual's ability to utilize semantic units in specific patterns, or syntactical units, to convey meaning. This communication skill is based on appropriate reception, discrimination, association, and memory skills which enable appropriate encoding of semantic and syntactic units and their relationships in providing effective communication skills. Through stimulation of the grammatical forms, the individual is familiarized with patterns with which he is able to express thoughts, actions, and feelings.

Task		Page
A	Choosing Correct Pronouns	95
B	Changing Proper Nouns to Pronouns	96
C	Choosing Possessive Forms	97
D	Generation of Possessive Forms	99
E	Formation of Possessives with Regular and Proper Nouns	102
F	Generation of Negative Statements	104
G	Generation of Negative Contractives	105
H	Choosing the Correct Comparative/Superlative Form	107
I	Completion of Comparative/Superlative Forms in Sentences	108
J	Fill-in-the-Blank for Regular Plurals	110
K	Sentence Completion for Regular Plurals	113
L	Discrimination and Generation of Alternate Singular/Plural Forms for Regular Nouns	115
M	Fill-in-the-Blank for Irregular Plurals	117
N	Sentence Completion for Irregular Plurals	119
O	Discrimination and Generation of Alternate Singular/Plural Forms for Irregular Nouns	121
P	Regular and Irregular Plurals — Mixed Forms	123
Q	Noun-Verb Agreement	125
R	Choosing the Correct Sentence for Present Progressive Verbs	128

S	Fill-in-the-Blank for Present Progressive Verbs	130
T	Choosing the Correct Sentence for Regular Past Tense Verbs	132
U	Fill-in-the-Blank for Regular Past Tense Verbs	134
V	Regular Past Tense Verbs: List	136
W	Choosing the Correct Sentence for Irregular Past Tense Verbs	138
X	Fill-in-the-Blank for Irregular Past Tense Verbs	140
Y	Irregular Past Tense Verbs: List	141
Z	Fill-in-the-Blank for Mixed Past Tense Verbs	143
AA	Choosing the Correct Sentence for Future Tense Verbs	144
BB	Fill-in-the-Blank for Future Tense Verbs	146
CC	Choosing the Correct Sentence with Mixed Verb Forms	148
DD	Fill-in-the-Blank for Mixed Verb Tenses	150
EE	Generation of Verb Tenses	151
FF	Rearranging Words to Form Correct and Complete Sentences	152
GG	Description of Common Objects	155
HH	Completion of Story Line	157

Grammar

Task A: Choosing Correct Pronouns

Circle the correct pronoun for each sentence. The first one is done for you.

1. ((She,) Her) is outside.
2. (Him, He) is the son of the mayor.
3. (She, Her) is a little girl.
4. (Them, They) went to school on Sunday.
5. (It, He) is a brown paper bag.
6. I saw (she, her) yesterday in the park.
7. Can you hear (we, us)?
8. (Us, We) can't go to the movies alone.
9. (Me, I) am afraid of lions and bears.
10. Can we sit with (they, them)?
11. (His, He) is coming over tonight.
12. Please give the book to her and (I, me).
13. John said he and (I, me) were going to the circus.
14. You and (me, I) are in the same class.
15. Mary gave (her, she) a bunch of clothes from the trunk.
16. (Him, He) can't stay after school today.
17. The stool fell on me and (him, he).
18. Grandma can fit (they, them) in the back seat.
19. (Us, We) are good children in church.
20. With the two of (us, we) working, the job was completed.
21. (Her, She) practiced her trumpet until late in the evening.
22. The boys helped (they, them) move the furniture.
23. Betty and (I, me) danced with the boys down the street.
24. Michael called (me, I) on the phone.

25. Can't you tell (them, they) to quiet down?

26. The old woman cooked dinner for (we, us) all.

27. I showed (her, she) how to do the homework.

28. The chair belongs to Mike and (I, me).

29. (They, Them) are boys from the reform school.

30. (Him, He) will open the car door if it isn't locked.

I.E.P. Goal: The client will select the correct pronoun in a sentence with 90% or greater accuracy.

Grammar
Task B: Changing Proper Nouns to Pronouns

Change the underlined proper noun in each sentence to a pronoun. The first one is done for you.

1. John is here. ___He___

2. Suzanne will come over later to help. _____

3. Give it to Mary, please. _____

4. Did you see Bill? _____

5. Becky went home after the show. _____

6. Jeremy is not feeling well tonight. _____

7. Sue and Jon live next door. _____

8. The car belongs to Al and Tom. _____

9. Mark and I are going to the play. _____

10. Charlie said he would not go today. _____

11. I gave Philip a new necktie. _____

12. The nuns gave the statue to Stuart and me. _____

13. Doug, Alice and I went to the movies. _____

14. James and Melanie took a vacation to Florida. _____

15. Give the money to Fred and me. _____

16. Can we go to the lake with Randy and Michelle? _____

17. The <u>Jones</u> gave us the use of their house. _____

18. <u>Margaret</u> bought the rocking chair for <u>Larry</u>. _____ _____

19. He helped <u>Pam</u> carry the books. _____

20. <u>Sam</u> and <u>Andrea</u> couldn't find the lost children. _____

21. <u>Carrie</u> bought the rug at a discount store. _____

22. <u>Charlie</u> is a true gentlemen. _____

23. Never tell <u>Penny</u> about the mysterious noise. _____

24. <u>Patrick</u> and <u>Rick</u> played all night long. _____

25. Please hand the racket to <u>Teresa</u> and <u>me</u>. _____

26. <u>Matthew</u> gave the ball to <u>Barbara</u>. _____ _____

27. <u>James</u>, <u>Ralph</u> and <u>I</u> went to the fish fry at the beach. _____

28. They called <u>Charlie</u> and <u>Betty</u> last night. _____

29. Don't let <u>Margaret</u> break it. _____

I.E.P. Goal: The client will change proper nouns to pronouns in sentences with 90% or greater accuracy.

Grammar
Task C: Choosing Possessive Forms

Circle the correct pronoun for each sentence. The first one is done for you.

1. It is (**my**, mine) bracelet.
2. I went to (they, their) house.
3. It's not (theirs, thems).
4. The bicycle is (our, ours).
5. It is (her, hers) dress.
6. The painting is (your, yours).
7. Mary, please give (my, mine) book to her.
8. (Our, Ours) friends were at the party.
9. I bought (him, his) necktie.
10. The razor was (his, hims).

11. The boy fixed (him, his) bicycle yesterday.

12. (My, Mine) father is a great person.

13. When you have finished, please return (our, ours) cards.

14. (Their, theirs) corn is cheaper than mine.

15. The market belongs to (her, hers).

16. (She, Her) car is in the garage.

17. (Your, Yours) membership was cancelled last month.

18. Michele had (my, mine) book at (her, hers) office.

19. I will come to (your, yours) house at eight o'clock.

20. (Her, Hers) sweater looks exactly like (my, mine).

21. The child fell and hurt (his, hims) finger.

22. (Their, Theirs) furniture has been stored in (my, mine) workshop.

23. The barbershop chair belongs to (her, she).

24. The T-shirt shop sold ten of (their, theirs) shirts.

25. That's (our, ours) father in the basement.

26. The record player belonged to (him, his).

27. It is (their, theirs) property on the lake.

28. Put (my, mine) boat in (their, theirs) garage.

29. (Her, Hers) bedroom suite was bought at (my, mine) store.

30. Those are (our, ours) lamps sitting on the table.

I.E.P. Goal: *The client will select the correct possessive pronoun in a sentence with 90% or greater accuracy.*

Grammar
Task D: Generation of Possessive Forms

Read the first sentence in each set. Complete the other sentences with a possessive pronoun. The first one in each set is done for you.

I.

1. The boy was given a brand new bicycle.

   The bicycle belongs to __*him*__. The bicycle is __*his*__.

2. For her birthday, Marie received a pencil set from her mother.

   The pencil set belongs to _____. The pencil set is _____.

3. The little girl had on a pink sweater.

   The sweater is _____. The sweater belongs to _____.

4. Mike and George saved their money and bought a wagon.

   The wagon belongs to _____. The wagon is _____.

5. In Teddy's room there is a set of battleships.

   The battleships are _____. The battleships belong to _____.

6. Helen's new sneakers were blue and white.

   The sneakers belong to _____. The sneakers are _____.

7. Martha bought a chair for the kitchen.

   The chair is _____. The chair belongs to _____.

8. Mark wrote a story for the school newspaper.

   The story belongs to _____. The story is _____.

9. The flowers were picked out of Mary's garden.

   The flowers are _____. The flowers belong to _____.

10. The tourists bought a tour map of the caverns.

    The map belongs to _____. The map is _____.

11. The children made cookies for the dinner.

    The cookies are _____. The cookies belong to _____.

12. We built a birdhouse in the oak tree.

    The birdhouse is _____. The birdhouse belongs to _____.

13. The girl earned a driver's license on Thursday.

    The license belongs to _____. The license is _____.

14. Sally bought a tennis racket.

    The racket belongs to _____. The racket is _____.

15. The basketball players bought hamburgers after the game.

    The hamburgers are _____. The hamburgers belong to _____.

16. The television set was given to us.

    The television set belongs to _____. The television set is _____.

17. David and George were given a pet monkey.

    The monkey belongs to _____. The monkey is _____.

18. Ned gave an engagement ring to Jane.

    The ring is _____. The ring belongs to _____.

19. Edna gave the couple a beautiful wedding present.

    The present belongs to _____. The present is _____.

20. The car dealer had twenty cars on the lot.

    The cars are _____. The cars belong to _____.

II.
 1. The food is ours. It belongs to __us__.
 2. The ring is mine. It belongs to _____.
 3. The cookies are yours. They belong to _____.
 4. The toys are theirs. They belong to _____.
 5. The book is his. It belongs to _____.
 6. The dress is hers. It belongs to _____.
 7. The sofa is yours. It belongs to _____.

8. The record player is his. It belongs to _____.

9. The scarves are hers. They belong to _____.

10. The microphones are theirs. They belong to _____.

11. The farm is theirs. It belongs to _____.

12. The paper is mine. It belongs to _____.

13. The jumper is hers. It belongs to _____.

14. The book belongs to him. It is _____.

15. The dress belongs to her. It is _____.

16. The tambourine belongs to them. It is _____.

17. The furniture belongs to us. It is _____.

18. The dog belongs to me. It is _____.

19. The cakes belong to you. They are _____.

20. The bear belongs to him. It is _____.

21. The orchard belongs to them. It is _____.

22. The house belongs to us. It is _____.

23. The pillowcases belong to you. They are _____.

24. The china belongs to her. It is _____.

25. The costumes are for me. They are _____.

26. The tests belong to them. They are _____.

27. The apartments belong to us. They are _____.

28. The racket belongs to him. It is _____.

29. The tablecloth was given to you. It is _____.

30. The pictures belong to us. They are _____.

I.E.P. Goal: Given an incomplete sentence, the client will complete the sentence with the correct possessive pronoun form with 90% or greater accuracy.

Grammar

Task E: Formation of Possessives with Regular and Proper Nouns

Read the first sentence. Complete the second sentence using the possessive form of the noun or proper noun. The first one is done for you.

1. Jack presented the award to the boy.

    The award is the ____*boy's*____.

2. The woman won the first place prize for her exhibit.

    The prize was the _____.

3. Carrie gave her mother a necklace.

    The necklace is her _____.

4. The girl bought a black slip.

    The slip is the _____.

5. Jerry accepted the trophy for the lady.

    The trophy is the _____.

6. The baby had an operation on her nose.

    The _____ nose was fine.

7. The wagon belongs to the son.

    The wheel fell off the _____ wagon.

8. I gave my ball to my sister.

    The ball is now my _____.

9. Margaret had four rabbits.

    The brown _____ fur was matted.

10. The child went for a walk in the park carrying his balloon.

    The _____ balloon flew away in the breeze.

11. The firefighter responded to the call.

    The _____ hands were burned by the heat.

12. The teacher was well liked by all the children.

    The children got together and washed the _____ board.

13. Pam gave the hunter a gun and a hunting jacket.

    The gun and jacket are the _____.

14. Lisa gave the mail carrier a present for Christmas.

    The present is the _____.

15. Our neighbor has a red pickup truck.

    My _____ truck rolled down the hill.

16. The book belongs to David.

    It is _____.

17. Becky bought a house today.

    It is _____ house.

18. Michael has a dog.

    The dog is _____.

19. Terry gave Mary a birthday cake.

    It was _____ birthday.

20. Douglas has a beautiful bird.

    You should go see _____ bird.

21. Jeremy bought a new station wagon.

    We all went driving in _____ new car.

22. I gave Zeke a scarf for Christmas.

    The scarf is _____.

23. Mrs. Smith has the best pies.

    The pies are _____.

24. Theresa dyed her hair yesterday.

    The hair is _____.

25. The computer belonged to Andrew.

    The computer is _____.

26. The manager gave the shirts to Joe.

    The shirts are _____.

27. The telephone company would not refund Don his money.

    The money was _____.

28. The teacher gave Johnny an *A*.

    The *A* was _____.

29. Becky, the engineer's wife, was given a new outfit for her birthday.

    The outfit was _____.

30. Linda was given a box of candy.

    The candy was _____.

I.E.P. Goal: Given an incomplete sentence, the client will complete the sentence using the possessive form of the noun with 90% or greater accuracy.

Grammar
Task F: Generation of Negative Statements

Change each sentence to a negative statement. The first one is done for you.

1. Tom is sitting on the wall. *Tom is not sitting on the wall.*
2. The door is open. _____
3. Albert will go to school tomorrow. _____
4. The car is rolling down the hill. _____
5. Michael is washing his car. _____
6. Johnny has finished his work. _____
7. The ball popped. _____
8. The tree has fallen down. _____
9. The paper carrier will call tomorrow. _____
10. Santa Claus will come on Christmas Day. _____

11. The girl jumped into the lake. _____

12. Barbara parted the girls' hair before rolling it. _____

13. The children have gone to the circus. _____

14. Mindy may go to the drugstore if she wishes. _____

15. He shall have the position. _____

16. I would have given some money for the project. _____

17. Daniel could call for you. _____

18. Jim had taken the boy to the doctor. _____

19. Linda and Emmy walked to the park. _____

20. The inheritance shall be his. _____

21. You should do the work yourself. _____

22. Ned handed the pipe to George. _____

23. I would go if Mom let me. _____

24. Edward could arrange for the room. _____

25. The tepee may fall over in the rain. _____

26. The bookshelves could be delivered today. _____

27. I have heard about the job. _____

28. I should go talk to her. _____

29. Ann had driven the car to the lake. _____

30. The store has sold one hundred copies of the book. _____

I.E.P. Goal: The client will create a negative statement from an affirmative statement with 90% or greater accuracy.

Grammar
Task G: Generation of Negative Contractives

Write the underlined words as a contraction. The first one is done for you.

1. Barbara <u>could not</u> go to the movies. ___*couldn't*___

2. Terry has not come home yet. _____

3. We should not drive in this weather. _____

4. Cory and Jenny have not arrived at the hotel. _____

5. The children would not go with the stranger. _____

6. I will not be able to call you later. _____

7. Cheryl did not want to go to work today. _____

8. Housewives do not like to scrub the floors. _____

9. David does not have a new razor. _____

10. We will not be attending the wedding. _____

11. Jose cannot come out to play today. _____

12. Sue was not at the meeting this afternoon. _____

13. We would not go unless we had to make an appearance. _____

14. I could not answer the phone. _____

15. We should not tease people. _____

16. John and Sally have not bought a house in town. _____

17. Jerome did not have the money for the deal. _____

18. Pam cannot get married this year. _____

19. We will not take vacation until the fall. _____

20. We were not invited to the ball. _____

21. He cannot take the job after all. _____

22. George has not been sick at all this year. _____

23. Jeff does not have to leave today. _____

24. He was not very happy with the news. _____

25. The children were not well. _____

I.E.P. Goal: Given sentence models, the client will create negative contractives from verb and not constructions with 90% or greater accuracy.

Grammar
Task H: Choosing the Correct Comparative/Superlative Form

Circle the correct adjective to complete each sentence. The first one is done for you.

1. The boat was (*bigger*, biggest) than most.
2. Michael was the (smaller, smallest) boy in the class.
3. The (farther, farthest) star from earth cannot be seen.
4. Sugar is the (sweeter, sweetest) thing I have.
5. Mark is (younger, youngest) than the other boys on the trip.
6. Mother is (sicker, sickest) than yesterday.
7. The Jones family is the (poorer, poorest) family in the city.
8. Silk is the (finer, finest) material in the store.
9. John is (older, oldest) than Jeff.
10. Phil's boss is (richer, richest) than he.
11. The pups were the (fatter, fattest) I've ever seen.
12. This house is the (wider, widest) house on the block.
13. The (taller, tallest) tree in the yard fell down in the storm.
14. Jason's son is (shorter, shortest) than Mason's daughter.
15. The (longer, longest) stretch of fence will be knocked down.
16. This refrigerator is (wider, widest) than my old one.
17. This boat is a lot (nicer, nicest) than the Smith's.
18. The (cheaper, cheapest) entree in the restaurant is twenty dollars.
19. The daffodil is the (prettier, prettiest) spring flower.
20. The chocolate cake was (gooder, better) than the vanilla.

21. Jan has (more, most) paper than anyone.

22. Andrew was the (younger, youngest) boy in the neighborhood.

23. Jeremiah received the (less, least) amount of money.

24. Amy has many marbles, but Sarah has even (more, most).

25. These apartments are the (better, best).

26. This dinner was (worse, worst) than the one last week.

27. Mike has a hundred books, but his wife has the (more, most).

28. Jerry is (more anxious, most anxious) than Tommy.

29. This is the (more, most) fun I've had in years.

30. Robert is the (more appreciative, most appreciative) of everyone's help.

I.E.P. Goal: The client will choose the correct comparative or superlative form in a sentence with 90% or greater accuracy.

Grammar
Task I: Completion of Comparative/Superlative Forms in Sentences

Fill in the blank with the correct form of the underlined word. The first one is done for you.

1. My house is <u>big</u>.

   His house is even ___*bigger*___. Their house is the very ___*biggest*___.

2. My car is <u>fast</u>.

   His car is even _____. Their car is the very _____.

3. My hair is <u>long</u>.

   His hair is even _____. Their hair is the very _____.

4. My garden is <u>small</u>.

   Her garden is even _____. Their garden is the very _____.

5. My stove is <u>hot</u>.

   Her stove is even _____. Their stove is the very _____.

6. My house is <u>near</u>.

   His house is even _____. Their house is the very _____.

7. My ribbon is short.

   Her ribbon is even _____. Their ribbon is the very _____.

8. My dog is smart.

   His dog is even _____. Their dog is the very _____.

9. My desk is old.

   Her desk is even _____. Their desk is the very _____.

10. My drink is cold.

    His drink is even _____. Their drinks are the very _____.

11. My floor is clean.

    Her floor is even _____. Their floor is the very _____.

12. My aunt is nice.

    His aunt is even _____. Their aunt is the very _____.

13. My tree is tall.

    Her tree is even _____. Their tree is the very _____.

14. My picture is wide.

    Her picture is even _____. Their picture is the very _____.

15. My friend is fat.

    His friend is even _____. Their friend is the very _____.

16. I am rich.

    She is even _____. They are the very _____.

17. My dish is dirty.

    Her dish is even _____. Their dishes are the very _____.

18. My door is narrow.

    His door is even _____. Their door is the very _____.

19. My skin is rough.

    Her skin is even _____. Their skin is the very _____.

Copyright © 1987 LinguiSystems, Inc.

20. My grass is wet.

   His grass is even _____. Their grass is the very _____.

21. My son is loud.

   Her son is even _____. Their son is the very _____.

22. My steak is thick.

   Her steak is _____. Their steaks are the _____.

23. My step is slippery.

   Her step is even _____. His step is the very _____.

24. My glue is strong.

   Her glue is even _____. Their glue is the very _____.

25. My book is good.

   Her book is even _____. Their book is the very _____.

26. This movie is bad.

   That movie is even _____. These movies are the very _____.

27. I have many pets.

   She has even _____. He has the very _____.

28. I have some pennies.

   She has even _____. He has the very _____.

29. This boy is handsome.

   This boy is even _____. This boy is the _____.

30. This food is nutritious.

   This food is even _____. This food is the _____.

I.E.P. Goal: The client will supply the comparative and superlative adjective forms with 90% or greater accuracy.

Grammar
Task J: Fill-in-the-Blank for Regular Plurals

Fill in the blank with the plural form of the noun from the first sentence. The first one is done for you.

1. I have a dog. You have two ____*dogs*____.

110   Copyright © 1987 LinguiSystems, Inc.

2. I have a hat. You have three _____.

3. I have a book. You have ten _____.

4. I have a chair. You have two _____.

5. I have a pencil. You have six _____.

6. I have a can. You have four _____.

7. I have an apple. You have eight _____.

8. I have a tree. You have twenty _____.

9. I have a rug. You have two _____.

10. I have a pillow. You have five _____.

11. I have a skunk. You have four _____.

12. I have a school. You have two _____.

13. I have a car. You have three _____.

14. I see a clown. You see two _____.

15. I have a gun. You have three _____.

16. I have a motorcycle. You have six _____.

17. I have a bell. You have ten _____.

18. I have a doll. You have five _____.

19. I have a television. You have nine _____.

20. I have a jar. You have six _____.

21. I have a dress. You have ten _____.

22. I have a cookie. You have a dozen _____.

23. I have a glove. You have a pair of _____.

24. I have a cup. You have a set of _____.

25. I have a flower. You have a bunch of _____.

26. I have a pen. You have a couple of _____.

27. I have a car. You have a fleet of _____.

28. I have a friend. You have a lot of _____.
29. I have a bottle. You have a case of _____.
30. I have a stamp. You have a collection of _____.
31. I have a brick. You have a load of _____.
32. I have a pickle. You have a barrel of _____.
33. I have a doughnut. You have a batch of _____.
34. I have a potato. You have seven _____.
35. I have a box. You have four _____.
36. I see a witch. You see nine _____.
37. I have a lunch. You have three _____.
38. I see a church. You see two _____.
39. I ate a radish. You ate ten _____.
40. I see a fox. You see twelve _____.
41. I took a quiz. You took eight _____.
42. I have a house. You have three _____.
43. I heard an echo. You heard two _____.
44. I met a hero. You met four _____.
45. I have a dish. You have twelve _____.
46. I have a glass. You have ten _____.
47. I have a pearl. You have a string of _____.
48. I have a pretzel. You have a box of _____.
49. I have an egg. You have a carton of _____.
50. I have a potato chip. You have a bag of _____.
51. I have a Lifesaver. You have a package of _____.
52. I have a jar of pickles. You have two _____.
53. I have a can of soup. You have three _____.

54. I have one sister-in-law. You have four _____.

55. I have a box of crackers. You have six _____.

56. I have a pile of leaves. You have two _____.

57. I have a stack of papers. You have nine _____.

58. I have a pocketful of money. You have two _____.

59. I have a bunch of bananas. You have six _____.

60. I have one brother-in-law. You have three _____.

I.E.P. Goal: The client will supply the plural form for regular nouns with 90% or greater accuracy.

Grammar
Task K: Sentence Completion for Regular Plurals

Circle the word to complete each sentence. The first one is done for you.

1. The children ate all of the (cookie, (cookies)).

2. My mom bought a chocolate (cake, cakes) for my birthday.

3. Eat all of your (bean, beans).

4. I like to play outside on a sunny (day, days).

5. Please open the (door, doors) for my sister and me.

6. My pair of (sock, socks) was very dirty.

7. The girl fried two (egg, eggs) in a skillet.

8. My chest of (drawers, drawer) is full of clothes.

9. The (lamp, lamps) is in the foyer.

10. The (teacher, teachers) grouped together for the strike.

11. The (chairs, chair) broke when the man sat down.

12. The boy's (leg, legs) was broken.

13. The (flower, flowers) smell pretty.

14. The baker made two dozen (pie, pies).

15. The (rug, rugs) slipped out from under me.

16. The load of (brick, bricks) fell over the embankment.

17. The (stamp, stamps) were falling off.

18. The (doughnut, doughnuts) were stale.

19. Mary gave ten (book, books) to the library.

20. The fleet of (car, cars) was shipped out yesterday.

21. The cook has ten (can of soups, cans of soup).

22. The bridesmaids picked up their (dress, dresses) last week.

23. The (jar of pickles, jars of pickles) was empty.

24. The department store bought a (television, televisions).

25. The bag of (potato, potatoes) was spoiled.

26. (Witch, Witches) are evil characters.

27. Michael's (watch, watches) is not working.

28. The box of (cracker, crackers) was eaten.

29. Good (friend, friends) are hard to find.

30. Please buy a dozen (doughnut, doughnuts) today.

31. Telephone (pole, poles) are frequently hit by lightning.

32. The man had numerous (stack of papers, stacks of papers) to sort.

33. I would like to buy a (dish, dishes) for a party.

34. The basketball (game, games) was over at eight.

35. Put the loaf of (bread, breads) in the truck.

36. The (chair, chairs) at the table are very old.

37. Teachers have a lot of (student, students).

38. An apple (tree, trees) fell down in the storm last night.

39. The men wanted to buy some (rifle, rifles).

40. Mother put two (pillow, pillows) on the bed.

41. The soldier kept watch for two (day, days).

42. (Trampoline, Trampolines) are fun.

43. My fiancé sent me a dozen (rose, roses) for my birthday.

44. I have two (sister-in-law, sisters-in-law).

45. The (envelope, envelopes) were lost in the mail.

46. The secretaries bought a new (typewriter, typewriters).

47. The sand (dune, dunes) were tall and white.

48. I wear (glass, glasses) to help me see.

49. The student studied for a (quiz, quizzes) to be given on Thursday.

50. The men brought each of their (gun, guns) with them.

I.E.P. Goal: The client will choose the correct singular or plural form of the word based on the context of the sentence with 90% or greater accuracy.

Grammar
Task L: Discrimination and Generation of Alternate Singular/Plural Forms for Regular Nouns

Read each word or sentence. On the blank to the left of the word or sentence, write S if the word is singular, or P if the word is plural. If the word or sentence is singular, write its plural form on the blank to the right. If the word or sentence is plural, write its singular form on the blank to the right. The first one is done for you.

s = singular; p = plural

Words

1. **S** house **houses**
2. ___ bus _____
3. ___ chairs _____
4. ___ players _____
5. ___ leg _____
6. ___ teacher _____
7. ___ flowers _____
8. ___ door _____
9. ___ pencils _____
10. ___ map _____
11. ___ apples _____
12. ___ pickle _____
13. ___ doughnuts _____
14. ___ cookies _____
15. ___ pockets _____
16. ___ boxes _____
17. ___ banana _____
18. ___ watches _____
19. ___ potato _____
20. ___ quiz _____
21. ___ dishes _____
22. ___ glasses _____

23. ___ socks _____
24. ___ sister-in-law _____
25. ___ pillows _____
26. ___ pile of leaves _____
27. ___ hoop _____
28. ___ pearls _____
29. ___ basket _____
30. ___ radishes _____
31. ___ desk _____
32. ___ chest _____
33. ___ basketballs _____
34. ___ trampolines _____
35. ___ secretary _____
36. ___ guns _____
37. ___ carpet _____
38. ___ barrel _____
39. ___ shirts _____
40. ___ weeds _____
41. ___ fingers _____
42. ___ picture _____
43. ___ cup _____
44. ___ crow _____
45. ___ chickens _____
46. ___ noses _____
47. ___ belts _____
48. ___ stereos _____
49. ___ couch _____
50. ___ foxes _____

Sentences

1. _P_ I saw the <u>witches</u> in the haunted house. ___witch___
2. ___ The <u>door</u> blew open during the thunderstorm. _____
3. ___ The chocolate <u>doughnuts</u> were delicious. _____
4. ___ The <u>teacher</u> is the nicest of all. _____
5. ___ The <u>windows</u> were fogged up. _____
6. ___ <u>Hairstyles</u> change over the years. _____
7. ___ The <u>carpenter</u> was here today. _____
8. ___ <u>Glasses</u> were found in the back yard. _____
9. ___ My <u>sister-in-law</u> will be coming tomorrow. _____
10. ___ My stamp <u>collection</u> is worth a great deal of money. _____
11. ___ <u>Foxes</u> are often used for sport in England. _____

12. ___ The <u>load of bricks</u> was delivered Monday. _____

13. ___ <u>Television sets</u> were auctioned at the store. _____

14. ___ The <u>painting</u> was a beautiful work of art. _____

15. ___ Dill <u>pickles</u> are my favorite. _____

16. ___ <u>Stacks of paper</u> were found in the bin. _____

17. ___ <u>Cans of soup</u> were found in the kitchen. _____

18. ___ Martha broke a <u>dish</u>. _____

19. ___ School <u>lunches</u> are not very expensive. _____

20. ___ <u>Lifesavers</u> are very tasty. _____

21. ___ I will buy some <u>flowers</u> when I go out. _____

22. ___ <u>Machines</u> help cut down on the work people do. _____

23. ___ <u>Shrubs</u> need water and light. _____

24. ___ Mark has a <u>pocketful</u> of money. _____

25. ___ A <u>pile of leaves</u> was left in the back yard. _____

26. ___ Pack the <u>blankets</u> away. _____

27. ___ <u>Clowns</u> entertain all day at the circus. _____

28. ___ A <u>rocking chair</u> was broken in the house. _____

29. ___ Ten <u>bunches of bananas</u> were delivered to the zoo. _____

30. ___ He fell asleep on the <u>couch</u>. _____

I.E.P. Goal: The client will differentiate between singular and plural forms of regular nouns by identifying the form of the target noun and supplying the alternate form with 90% or greater accuracy.

Note: This activity may be expanded by having the client make up a sentence with the same meaning, substituting only the singular or plural form (the alternate of the one presented in the statement) and changing the verb form when necessary.

Grammar
Task M: Fill-in-the-Blank for Irregular Plurals

Fill in the blank with the plural form of the irregular noun from the first sentence. The first one is done for you.

1. I have a foot. You have two *feet*.

2. I have a goose. You have three _____.

3. I have a mouse. You have ten _____.
4. I see a leaf. You see twelve _____.
5. I have one loaf of bread. You have four _____ of bread.
6. I have a knife. You have two _____.
7. I see my wife. They see their _____.
8. I have a shelf. You have four _____.
9. I saw a thief. You saw three _____.
10. I saw an elf. You saw six _____.
11. I have a roof. You have two _____.
12. The tribe has a chief. This tribe has three _____.
13. He is a dwarf. There are ten _____.
14. I have a belief. You have many _____.
15. I have a scarf. You have twelve _____.
16. I saw a wolf. You saw six _____.
17. I have a calf. You have twenty _____.
18. I have a child. You have two _____.
19. I see a man. You see two _____.
20. I see an ox. You see two _____.
21. I see a woman. You see three _____.
22. I have a bar of soap. You have seven bars of _____.
23. I see a deer. You see two _____.
24. I see a moose. You see five _____.
25. I have a sheep. You have ten _____.
26. I have a fish. You have eight _____.
27. I am an alumnus. They are _____.
28. I have one datum. They have a lot of _____.

29. I lost one tooth. You lost ten _____.

30. I have some information. They have a lot of _____.

I.E.P. Goal: The client will supply the plural forms for irregular nouns with 90% or greater accuracy.

Grammar
Task N: Sentence Completion for Irregular Plurals

Complete each sentence by circling the correct singular or plural noun that fits the meaning of the sentence. The first one is done for you.

1. The boy fell and hurt his right ((foot), feet).
2. The flock of (sheep, sheeps) wandered across the pasture.
3. A (leaf, leaves) fell off the tree.
4. The baker made ten (loaf, loaves) of bread.
5. The boy's (tooth, teeth) were falling out.
6. There were three (goose, geese) in the barn yard.
7. A (knife, knives) was lost in the woods.
8. The three (woman, women) could not hear the speaker.
9. Santa Claus has (elf, elves) to help him make toys at Christmas.
10. The (roof, roofs) blew off the house during the storm.
11. The ten Indian (chief, chiefs) smoked the peace pipe.
12. The (moose, meese) were frightened by the spectators.
13. The wagon was pulled by two (ox, oxen).
14. A classroom has approximately twenty (childs, children) in it.
15. The (calf, calves) was lost without its mother.
16. The (fish, fishes) swam in a school.
17. The girl's (scarf, scarves) was red and white.
18. The young children had the (measle, measles).
19. John Brice bought an (ox, oxen) at the fair.
20. The twelve (fireman, firemen) battled the fire all night long.
21. Mark will take (mathematic, mathematics) in the fall.

22. The (dwarf, dwarfs) were very kind.

23. In most states a man cannot have two (wifes, wives).

24. The seven (deers, deer) ran through the woods.

25. Please put the ten (bookshelfs, bookshelves) up today.

26. The (mouses, mice) are growing in number.

27. Two hundred people lost their (lifes, lives) in the fire.

28. How many (deer, deers) did you see?

29. (Moose, Mooses) are unusual animals.

30. The (policeman, policemen) are funding the volunteer band.

31. The dentist pulled five (tooths, teeth).

32. The (gentleman, gentlemen) all came to the meeting.

33. Please hand me the bars of (soaps, soap).

34. The herd of (sheep, sheeps) slept on the hillside.

35. (Wolf, Wolves) are ferocious animals.

36. The (gooses, geese) were swimming on the lake.

37. (Childs, Children) like to play outdoors.

38. I saw a (calf, calves) a few minutes ago.

39. My new shoes make my (foot, feet) feel uncomfortable.

40. The (thief, thieves) were dressed up like dancers.

I.E.P. Goal: Based on the context of the sentence, the client will select the singular or plural irregular form with 90% or greater accuracy.

Grammar

Task O: Discrimination and Generation of Alternate Singular/Plural Forms for Irregular Nouns

Read each word or sentence. On the blank to the left of the word or sentence, write S if the word is singular, or P if the word is plural. If the word or sentence is singular, write its plural form on the blank to the right. If the word or sentence is plural, write its singular form on the blank to the right. The first one is done for you.

s = singular; p = plural

Words

1. __P__ children __child__
2. ___ moose _____
3. ___ mice _____
4. ___ teeth _____
5. ___ ox _____
6. ___ feet _____
7. ___ man _____
8. ___ soap _____
9. ___ sheep _____
10. ___ elf _____
11. ___ knives _____
12. ___ leaves _____
13. ___ information _____
14. ___ women _____
15. ___ firemen _____
16. ___ shelves _____
17. ___ deer _____
18. ___ loaf _____
19. ___ wife _____
20. ___ goose _____
21. ___ scarves _____
22. ___ thief _____
23. ___ roof _____
24. ___ wolves _____
25. ___ fish _____
26. ___ chief _____
27. ___ beliefs _____
28. ___ calves _____
29. ___ datum _____
30. ___ alumnus _____

Sentences

1. __P__ The policemen were talking over the C.B. __policeman__
2. ___ The tooth was lost in the pillow. _____
3. ___ The deer were running across the field. _____
4. ___ I saw a goose on the lake. _____
5. ___ The leaves are beautiful this time of year. _____

Copyright © 1987 LinguiSystems, Inc.

6. ___ I heard a pack of <u>wolves</u> last night. _____
7. ___ The <u>sheep</u> is grazing in the grass. _____
8. ___ The <u>knife</u> is made of heavy metal and has a wooden handle. _____
9. ___ The <u>datum</u> was incorrect. _____
10. ___ <u>Oxen</u> are useful animals for hauling. _____
11. ___ <u>Women</u> make up a major portion of the work force. _____
12. ___ The <u>thief</u> stole the expensive furs. _____
13. ___ Mark received the <u>information</u> for the project. _____
14. ___ Please buy a <u>loaf</u> of bread. _____
15. ___ The <u>roofs</u> were blown off in the storm. _____
16. ___ The <u>alumni</u> returned for the homecoming game. _____
17. ___ My <u>feet</u> are killing me! _____
18. ___ The <u>calf</u> wandered into the canyon. _____
19. ___ The man's <u>wife</u> jumped to her feet. _____
20. ___ The <u>soap</u> slipped out of the tub. _____
21. ___ The church's <u>beliefs</u> are varied. _____
22. ___ The <u>mice</u> crawled through the hole. _____
23. ___ <u>Children</u> can make a home happy. _____
24. ___ The <u>man</u> left town on the first train. _____
25. ___ <u>Fish</u> were seen in the lagoon. _____
26. ___ The <u>firemen</u> had a picnic. _____
27. ___ The <u>scarf</u> hung loosely around her neck. _____
28. ___ The <u>mailman</u> brought the mail at noon. _____
29. ___ The <u>moose</u> was standing on the hillside. _____
30. ___ <u>Elves</u> are used in cookie commercials. _____

I.E.P. Goal: The client will differentiate between singular and plural forms of irregular nouns by identifying the form of the target noun and supplying the alternate form with 90% or greater accuracy.

Grammar

Task P: Regular and Irregular Plurals - Mixed Forms

Regular and irregular noun plurals are mixed together in this task. Fill in the blank to complete each sentence. The first one is done for you.

1. My mother gave me a <u>pearl</u> which I had made into a string of ___pearls___.

2. I have one record <u>player</u> and you have two record _____.

3. I have a <u>horse</u> and my neighbor has ten _____.

4. I had three <u>dolls</u>. You gave me one, so now I have four _____.

5. The <u>oxen</u> grazed in the lower field and left the baby _____ by himself.

6. You had two <u>candy bars</u>. You gave one to your sister and kept one candy _____.

7. Yesterday, I ate an <u>apple</u>. I enjoyed it so much that I picked two bushels of _____.

8. One <u>goose</u> swam while three other _____ ate.

9. I put one <u>stamp</u> on the letter and four _____ on the package.

10. I only had one <u>shelf</u> so I bought three more _____ for my study.

11. The pink <u>dress</u> was so pretty I wanted the blue and red _____, too!

12. I went to the store to buy a <u>can</u> of soup and ended up buying five _____ of soup.

13. A tribe usually has one <u>chief</u>, but the Sioux tribe has six _____.

14. The frozen <u>loaf</u> of bread was fresh, but the other _____ were stale.

15. The master <u>thief</u> joined a gang of _____ to plan a major robbery.

Read the list of words. Mark whether each one is singular or plural. Then write the word in the opposite way on the blank. The first one is done for you.

1. _P_ pies ___pie___   2. ___ women _____

3. ___ oxen _____
4. ___ potato _____
5. ___ wife _____
6. ___ father _____
7. ___ windows _____
8. ___ chair _____
9. ___ door _____
10. ___ mice _____
11. ___ moose _____
12. ___ house _____
13. ___ dresses _____
14. ___ policemen _____
15. ___ geese _____
16. ___ leaf _____

17. ___ flowers _____
18. ___ sheep _____
19. ___ shelves _____
20. ___ foot _____
21. ___ jets _____
22. ___ sisters-in-law _____
23. ___ alumnus _____
24. ___ heroes _____
25. ___ wolf _____
26. ___ cake _____
27. ___ branches _____
28. ___ soap _____
29. ___ fish _____
30. ___ firemen _____

Read the sentences. Mark whether the underlined word is singular or plural. Then write the word in the opposite way on the blank. The first one is done for you.

1. _P_ My <u>friends</u> do everything with me. __friend__
2. ___ My dentist extracted my <u>tooth</u> today. _____
3. ___ Let's try to catch the <u>moose</u>. _____
4. ___ The <u>pencil set</u> is one of the nicest I've seen. _____
5. ___ The <u>children</u> liked to climb the trees. _____
6. ___ The <u>leaves</u> fall off in the fall. _____
7. ___ The <u>deer</u> leaped easily over the fence. _____
8. ___ The <u>mouse</u> was hungry. _____
9. ___ The <u>scarves</u> were sold at half price. _____
10. ___ Please lock the <u>house</u> before you leave. _____
11. ___ Margaret has a <u>brother-in-law</u> in Texas. _____

124   Copyright © 1987 LinguiSystems, Inc.

12. ___ The monkey ate a <u>bunch</u> of bananas. _____

13. ___ The <u>doughnuts</u> tasted stale. _____

14. ___ My <u>beliefs</u> do not change often. _____

15. ___ The <u>dishes</u> in the sink were dirty. _____

16. ___ The <u>man</u> got away from the police. _____

17. ___ Santa Claus has many <u>elves</u>. _____

18. ___ I brought many <u>boxes</u> with me. _____

19. ___ The <u>fish</u> were swimming away. _____

20. ___ The <u>dress</u> was just my size. _____

I.E.P. Goal: The client will form the singular and plural forms of regular and irregular nouns when both forms are presented together with 90% or greater accuracy.

Grammar
Task Q: Noun-Verb Agreement

Circle the word that correctly completes each sentence. The first one is done for you.

1. The boys (is, **are**) going to school.
2. Mary Sue (was, were) crying in her room.
3. Jennifer and Johnny (was, were) playing ball.
4. Philip (has, have) a lot of work to do.
5. The twins (was, were) riding their bicycles.
6. The wooden chair (is, are) rotten.
7. The class (was, were) reading a book.
8. Dick and his wife (is, are) taking a trip.
9. The tables (was, were) turned over.
10. Matthew (has, have) a riding lesson this Thursday.
11. The fire (was, were) burning brightly.
12. Melinda (is, are) studying for her test.
13. The students (has, have) been taking pictures this week.
14. Barbara and the children (is, are) baking cookies.

15. The trees (is, are) blowing in the wind.

16. (Has, Have) you ever ridden a roller coaster?

17. (Is, Are) you ready to go riding?

18. The light switch (is, are) turned on.

19. The cups (is, are) in the cupboard.

20. Mary (walk, walks) every evening before dinner.

21. Martin and Pam (was, were) going to the beach.

22. John (is, are) getting engaged this weekend.

23. Charlie (is, are) my friend.

24. The children (sleep, sleeps) soundly after a hard day.

25. He (is, are) in the basement.

26. The clowns (was, were) funny.

27. The boy (walk, walks) to school.

28. The dog (was, were) barking this morning.

29. We (is, are) here on time.

30. The lady (was, were) late to her appointment.

31. The man (was, were) angry with his two sons.

32. She (do, does) a good job.

33. The books (was, were) at the library.

34. The baby (is, are) happy.

35. The shoe (was, were) missing.

36. The cookies (is, are) still warm from the oven.

37. The drink (is, are) cold.

38. Our cat (likes, like) to ride in the car.

39. The boy (goes, go) to school.

40. Marty (do, does) his chores after supper.

41. Where (do, does) your mom work?

42. I (has, have) to go home now.

43. Clarence (was, were) giving a show tonight.

44. The man (is, are) nice to the children.

45. What (has, have) you done with my balloon?

46. We don't (has, have) enough time.

47. Does that girl (has, have) a dress like yours?

48. Sherrie (has, have) a bad cold today.

49. I think they (has, have) an older brother.

50. Janet (do, does) her homework.

51. The birds (fly, flies) south in the winter.

52. The pilot (check, checks) all the controls before takeoff.

53. Don't (ride, rides) your bicycle in a busy street.

54. Mother (drive, drives) the car to work.

55. The geese (waddle, waddles) to the other side of the yard.

56. Please (write, writes) me soon.

57. I like to (hike, hikes) on weekends.

58. The couple (run, runs) every night.

59. Jeff (read, reads) horror stories at night.

60. The baseball players (hit, hits) practice balls.

61. The twins (is, are) having a good time.

62. (Has, Have) you been to the candy store?

63. The brown rug (look, looks) worn out.

64. Ted and Joan (is, are) going to the festival.

65. Jeremy (want, wants) the new job.

66. The shells (is, are) all over the beach.

67. The television shows (was, were) entertaining.

68. Todd (likes, like) to water ski.

69. My fiancé (call, calls) me every night.

70. The school (admit, admits) hundreds of students.

71. My father (open, opens) the store every day.

72. The mail carrier (bring, brings) me letters.

73. Teachers (assign, assigns) homework for the students.

74. Taxi cabs (take, takes) you to your destination.

75. Candlesticks (is, are) nice gifts.

I.E.P. Goal: The client will choose the singular or plural verb form based on the context of the sentence with 90% or greater accuracy.

Grammar
Task R: Choosing the Correct Sentence for Present Progressive Verbs

Put a check beside the sentence in each set that is correct. The first one is done for you.

1. ✓ The girl is walking to the store.
   ___ The girl walk to the store.

2. ___ The boys is playing ball today.
   ___ The boys are playing ball today.

3. ___ The bird fall out of the tree.
   ___ The bird is falling out of the tree.

4. ___ They are going to get caught if they aren't careful.
   ___ They is going to get caught if they aren't careful.

5. ___ The cord break with the strain.
   ___ The cord is breaking with the strain.

6. ___ Madeline go to the concert tonight.
   ___ Madeline is going to the concert tonight.

7. ___ Marty and Joannie are having a party.
   ___ Marty and Joannie is having a party.

8. ___ The jukebox is playing old hit records.
   ___ The jukebox play old hit records.

9. ___ Terry is not catching the ball.
   ___ Terry is not catch the ball.

10. ___ The police officer are ride the motorcycle.
    ___ The police officer is riding the motorcycle.

11. ___ The building is burning.
    ___ The building are burning.

12. ___ The washing machine is washed the clothes.
    ___ The washing machine is washing the clothes.

13. ___ The rocket is not falling from the sky.
    ___ The rocket not fall from the sky.

14. ___ She is reading the book.
    ___ She are reading the book.

15. ___ Mark is missing his test tonight.
    ___ Mark is miss his test tonight.

16. ___ I is jumping into the pool.
    ___ I am jumping into the pool.

17. ___ The clock is ticking.
    ___ The clock are ticking.

18. ___ The temperature is falling.
    ___ The temperature is falled.

19. ___ Betsy is going to the beach today.
    ___ Betsy is went to the beach today.

20. ___ James is crying because he lost his dog.
    ___ James has crying because he lost his dog.

21. ___ The police officer is stopped the cars.
    ___ The police officer is stopping the cars.

22. ___ The boys is swimming in the pond.
    ___ The boys are swimming in the pond.

23. ___ The artist is painting the picture in his gallery.
    ___ The artist am painting the picture in his gallery.

24. ___ The farmer is plant the seeds in his field.
    ___ The farmer is planting the seeds in his field.

25. ___ The horse is neighing.
    ___ The horse is neigh.

I.E.P. Goal: The client will identify sentences with correct present progressive verb forms with 90% or greater accuracy.

Grammar

Task S: Fill-in-the-Blank for Present Progressive Verbs

Read the first sentence in each set. The first sentence describes what someone or something usually does or likes to do. Fill in the blanks of the last sentence with words that say what is happening right now. The first word will be either *is* or *are*. The first one is done for you.

1. Betty likes to eat.

    Now she *is* *eating* .

2. Sue likes to sew.

    Now she _____ _____.

3. The dog likes to jump.

    Now it _____ _____.

4. The bell can ring.

    Now it _____ _____.

5. Birds like to sing.

    The birds _____ _____.

6. Harry likes to walk.

    Here he _____ _____.

7. Joann likes to hop.

    In the schoolyard, Joann _____ _____.

8. Buster likes to talk.

    Now he _____ _____.

9. Barry likes to read.

    Here he _____ _____.

10. James always studies.

    Now he _____ _____.

11. Fred runs. What is he doing?

    He _____ _____.

12. We talk. What are we doing?

    We _____ _____.

13. They drive. What are they doing?

    They _____ _____.

14. Babies cry. What are they doing?

    They _____ _____.

15. Mary thinks. What is she doing?

    She _____ _____.

16. Chimes ring. What are they doing?

    They _____ _____.

17. Carla writes. What is she doing?

    She _____ _____.

18. Tony flies airplanes. What is he doing?

    He _____ _____ an airplane.

19. Bookstores sell books. What are they doing?

    They _____ _____ books.

20. Jerry waters flowers. What is he doing?

    He _____ _____ flowers.

21. The fire burns. What is it doing?

    It _____ _____.

22. Some people marry. What are they doing?

    They _____ _____.

23. John likes to sleep. What is he doing?

    He _____ _____.

24. Children like to play. What are they doing?

    They _____ _____.

Copyright © 1987 LinguiSystems, Inc.

25. The man <u>shoots</u> arrows. What is he doing?

   He _____ _____ arrows.

26. Melanie likes to <u>type</u>. What is she doing?

   She _____ _____.

27. Linda <u>jogs</u> and <u>swims</u>. What is Linda doing?

   Linda _____ _____ and _____.

28. Jeffrey likes to <u>sail</u> and <u>fish</u>. What is Jeffrey doing?

   Jeffrey _____ _____ and _____.

29. The baby <u>laughs</u> and <u>plays</u>. What is the baby doing?

   The baby _____ _____ and _____.

30. Lisa <u>types</u> and <u>files</u>. What is Lisa doing?

   Lisa _____ _____ and _____.

I.E.P. Goal: The client will supply correct singular and plural present progressive verb forms with 90% or greater accuracy.

Grammar
Task T: Choosing the Correct Sentence for Regular Past Tense Verbs

Read each set of sentences. Put a check beside the sentence that describes something that has already happened. The first one is done for you.

1. ✓ The boy walked home.
   ___ The boy walk home.

2. ___ I washing the car.
   ___ I washed the car.

3. ___ She opens the letter.
   ___ She opened the letter.

4. ___ The boys done ate their lunch.
   ___ The boys ate their lunch.

5. ___ John helped me with my homework.
   ___ John help me with my homework.

6. ___ He pushing the door open.
   ___ He pushed the door open.

7. __ He laughed at the story.
   __ He is laughing at the story.

8. __ Bertha is watch television.
   __ Bertha watched television.

9. __ The baby crawling up the steps.
   __ The baby crawled up the steps.

10. __ The boy is kicked the ball.
    __ The boy kicked the ball.

11. __ The children cried at the news.
    __ The children cry at the news.

12. __ The mothers is talking about the children.
    __ The mothers talked about the children.

13. __ Penny jumped over the hurdle.
    __ Penny had jump over the hurdle.

14. __ Michael shout during the game.
    __ Michael shouted during the game.

15. __ The gentleman tipped his hat.
    __ The gentleman tip his hat.

16. __ The salesclerk deliver the boxes yesterday.
    __ The salesclerk delivered the boxes yesterday.

17. __ Marcia jumped when she saw the spider.
    __ Marcia jump when she saw the spider.

18. __ The children skipped to school.
    __ The children is skip to school.

19. __ The ballerinas danced at the recital.
    __ The ballerinas are dance at the recital.

20. __ The school children waited for the bus.
    __ The school children are wait for the bus.

21. __ The kitchen help cooked the dinner.
    __ The kitchen help is cook the dinner.

22. __ We listen to the radio program yesterday.
    __ We listened to the radio program yesterday.

23. __ Jeremy hop on the green grass.
    __ Jeremy hopped on the green grass.

24. ___ The firefighter saved the child.
    ___ The firefighter save the child.

25. ___ Kevin crawled under the table.
    ___ Kevin crawl under the table.

26. ___ Linda paint the window frame.
    ___ Linda painted the window frame.

27. ___ Dan pushed the wagon down the road.
    ___ Dan push the wagon down the road.

28. ___ Tom chew the gum yesterday.
    ___ Tom chewed the gum yesterday.

29. ___ Paul swallow pills with water.
    ___ Paul swallowed pills with water.

30. ___ Tim rested under the oak tree.
    ___ Tim rest under the oak tree.

I.E.P. Goal: The client will identify regular past tense verb forms with 90% or greater accuracy.

Grammar
Task U: Fill-in-the-Blank for Regular Past Tense Verbs

The first sentence in each set describes something that is about to happen. Fill in the blank of the second sentence that tells that the event has already happened. The first one is done for you.

1. Claire was going to smile. I saw her when she __*smiled*__.

2. Ralph was going to mow the grass. This is the grass that he _____.

3. Tom was going to chop the logs. These are the logs that he _____.

4. Carrie was going to dance. We saw her when she _____.

5. The children were going to laugh. We heard them when they _____.

6. We were going to wait for the bus. We stood and _____.

7. Mom was going to bake some cookies. We ate all the cookies that she _____.

8. The children were going to skip. We saw them as they _____.

9. Nelson was going to look. This is where he _____.

10. Otto was going to push the wagon. This is the wagon that he _____.

11. He was going to watch a TV show. This is the show that he _____.

12. Maria was going to jump the hurdle. This is the hurdle that she _____.

13. David was going to rest under the tree. Here is where he _____.

14. Thelma was going to swallow the pills. These are the pills that she _____.

15. Eric was going to chew the gum. This is the gum that he _____.

16. Jeff was going to crawl in the dirt. This is where he _____.

17. Sam was going to open the letter. This is the letter that he _____.

18. The boys were going to kick the ball. This is the ball that they _____.

19. The children were going to skate. We watched them when they _____.

20. Willie was going to work in the garden. This is the garden where he _____.

21. Ian was about to trip over the doorjamb. This is the doorjamb where he _____.

22. Selise was going to climb the tree. This is the tree that she _____.

23. Harry was going to mix the cement. This is the cement that he _____.

24. Sherrie was going to skin her knee. This is the knee that she _____.

25. The clock was going to stop. This is the clock that _____.

26. The Wilsons were going to move. This is the house where they

   _____.

27. Jan was going to wash the clothes. These are the clothes that she

   _____.

28. Emmy was going to marry Dick. Dick is the man she _____.

29. Carrie was going to drop the shoe. This is the shoe that she _____.

30. Max was going to miss the movie. This is the movie that he _____.

I.E.P. goal: The client will form regular past tense verb forms based on the context of the sentence with 90% or greater accuracy.

Grammar
Task V: Regular Past Tense Verbs: List

The past tense of each verb below is formed by adding an *ed* to the verb. On the blank beside each verb, write the past tense form. Remember that if the verb ends in *y*, the *y* sometimes changes to *i* when you add the *ed*. The first one is done for you.

1. ask *asked*
2. attach _____
3. bathe _____
4. carry _____
5. chop _____
6. clean _____
7. climb _____
8. cook _____
9. crawl _____
10. cry _____
11. dance _____
12. dock _____
13. drop _____
14. fill _____
15. fix _____

16. gather _____
17. guess _____
18. hug _____
19. joke _____
20. jump _____
21. kick _____
22. knock _____
23. laugh _____
24. listen _____
25. love _____
26. mail _____
27. marry _____
28. miss _____
29. mix _____
30. move _____

31. mow _____
32. need _____
33. nod _____
34. pack _____
35. paint _____
36. peek _____
37. pick _____
38. place _____
39. play _____
40. pull _____
41. push _____
42. race _____
43. rain _____
44. rake _____
45. reach _____
46. remember _____
47. seem _____
48. shift _____
49. shout _____
50. sip _____
51. skate _____
52. skim _____
53. skip _____

54. smile _____
55. smoke _____
56. spray _____
57. stay _____
58. stop _____
59. talk _____
60. tease _____
61. thank _____
62. tip _____
63. trip _____
64. turn _____
65. vote _____
66. wait _____
67. walk _____
68. warn _____
69. wash _____
70. waste _____
71. watch _____
72. wax _____
73. work _____
74. worry _____
75. zip _____

I.E.P. Goal: The client will supply the past tense forms of regular verbs with 90% or greater accuracy.

Grammar

Task W: Choosing the Correct Sentence for Irregular Past Tense Verbs

Some verbs change their spelling when they change to the past tense. Read the sets of sentences below. Put a check beside the sentence with the correct past tense verb form. The first one is done for you.

1. ✓ Mary drank her chocolate milk.
   ___ Mary drunk her chocolate milk.

2. ___ The girls chose the costumes.
   ___ The girls choosed the costumes.

3. ___ Michael drived the car.
   ___ Michael drove the car.

4. ___ The ice froze.
   ___ The ice freezed.

5. ___ The window broked.
   ___ The window broke.

6. ___ Jamie throwed the ball.
   ___ Jamie threw the ball.

7. ___ The thieves stealed the bicycle.
   ___ The thieves stole the bicycle.

8. ___ The model wore the pink dress.
   ___ The model weared the pink dress.

9. ___ The class writed the play.
   ___ The class wrote the play.

10. ___ The children went on a field trip.
    ___ The children goes on a field trip.

11. ___ He gived to the United Way.
    ___ He gave to the United Way.

12. ___ The boy growed three inches.
    ___ The boy grew three inches.

13. ___ The teacher rang the bell.
    ___ The teacher ringed the bell.

14. ___ He spoke for the children.
    ___ He speaked for the children.

15. ___ The bird flied away.
    ___ The bird flew away.

16. ___ He drew the beautiful picture.
    ___ He drawed the beautiful picture.

17. ___ Gerald digged the hole.
    ___ Gerald dug the hole.

18. ___ The old man built the house.
    ___ The old man builded the house.

19. ___ Thomas sitted in the chair.
    ___ Thomas sat in the chair.

20. ___ The children blowed the candles out.
    ___ The children blew the candles out.

21. ___ Mick stood at the end of the aisle.
    ___ Mick standed at the end of the aisle.

22. ___ Betty ran down the street.
    ___ Betty runned down the street.

23. ___ The squirrel breaked the stick.
    ___ The squirrel broke the stick.

24. ___ Amos slept all day long.
    ___ Amos sleeped all day long.

25. ___ I awaked to the sound of popcorn.
    ___ I awoke to the sound of popcorn.

26. ___ I speaked to him about that.
    ___ I spoke to him about that.

27. ___ The thief stole the car.
    ___ The thief stealed the car.

28. ___ I bringed it to you yesterday.
    ___ I brought it to you yesterday.

29. ___ The pilot flew the airplane through the sky.
    ___ The pilot flied the airplane through the sky.

30. ___ Larry gaved her a ring last night.
    ___ Larry gave her a ring last night.

I.E.P. Goal: *The client will identify irregular past tense verb forms when they are used in sentences with 90% or greater accuracy.*

Grammar
Task X: Fill-in-the-Blank for Irregular Past Tense Verbs

Answer each question below using the correct past tense verb form. Hint! You will have to change the spelling! The first one is done for you.

1. The squirrel was hiding some nuts. Where are the nuts that he ___*hid*___?

2. The girl was going to sleep upstairs. Show me the room where she _____.

3. Were you going to feed both dogs? Which ones have you _____?

4. The man was going to run five miles. This is the course where he _____.

5. Harry is going to bend the wire. Now the wire has been _____.

6. She is going to buy a new dress. This is the dress that she _____.

7. We are going to eat a sandwich. That's not the sandwich that we _____.

8. The children are going to see a movie. That is the movie they _____.

9. I was going to throw the ball. This is the ball that I _____.

10. Terry was going to swim. This is the pool where he _____.

11. The football team hoped to win the game. This is the game that they _____.

12. Jake is going to write a book. This is the book that he _____.

13. The gentleman is going to speak at the dinner. This is the place where he _____.

14. Paul is going to drive the car. This is the car that he _____.

15. Deborah is going to give Max a book. This is the book that she _____.

16. The movie is going to begin. This is the movie that _____.

17. The pilot is going to fly the plane. This is the plane that he _____.

18. The farmer is going to grow some corn. This is the corn that he _____.

19. The thief is going to steal the jewels. These are the jewels that he _____.

20. The boy is going to ring the bell. This is the bell that he _____.

21. Margaret is going to break the stick. This is the stick that she _____.

22. The girl was going to draw a picture. This is the picture that she _____.

23. I was going to eat her cake. This is the cake that I _____.

24. He is going to forget the appointment. This is the appointment that he _____.

25. The sun is going to rise in the morning. This is the time that it _____.

26. The young girl is going to lie down. This is where she _____.

27. Ned is going to drink the milk. This is the milk that he _____.

28. The boy is going to slide down the hill. This is the hill where he _____.

29. The woman is going to get a telegram. This is the telegram that she _____.

30. Tim is going to choose the game. This is the game that he _____.

I.E.P. Goal: The client will supply the past tense form of irregular verbs with 90% or greater accuracy.

Grammar
Task Y: Irregular Past Tense Verbs: List

The past tense of each of these verbs is formed by changing the spelling of the word. On the blank beside each word, write the past tense form. Be sure to check your spelling. The first one is done for you.

1. begin __*began*__
2. blow _____
3. break _____
4. bring _____
5. build _____
6. buy _____
7. catch _____
8. choose _____
9. come _____
10. cut _____
11. dig _____
12. dive _____
13. do _____
14. draw _____
15. drink _____
16. drive _____
17. eat _____
18. fall _____
19. feed _____
20. feel _____
21. fight _____
22. find _____

23. fly _____
24. forget _____
25. forgive _____
26. freeze _____
27. get _____
28. give _____
29. go _____
30. grow _____
31. have _____
32. hide _____
33. hit _____
34. hold _____
35. keep _____
36. know _____
37. lead _____
38. leap _____
39. leave _____
40. lend _____
41. lie _____
42. make _____
43. meet _____
44. read _____
45. ride _____
46. ring _____
47. rise _____

48. run _____
49. say _____
50. see _____
51. sell _____
52. shoot _____
53. shrink _____
54. sing _____
55. sink _____
56. sit _____
57. speak _____
58. spin _____
59. spring _____
60. stand _____
61. steal _____
62. stink _____
63. sweep _____
64. swim _____
65. take _____
66. teach _____
67. tear _____
68. tell _____
69. think _____
70. throw _____
71. wear _____
72. weave _____

73. win _____   75. write _____

74. wind _____

I.E.P. Goal: *The client will supply irregular past tense verb forms with 90% or greater accuracy.*

Grammar
Task Z: Fill-in-the-Blank for Mixed Past Tense Verbs

Fill in the blank with the correct past tense verb. The present tense form of the verb is written beside each sentence. The first one is done for you.

1. forget   I was late to school today and ____*forgot*____ my books.
2. give   The boy _____ the ball to her last week.
3. break   Someone _____ the mirror.
4. cook   The young woman _____ the vegetables.
5. crawl   The soldiers _____ through the obstacle course.
6. choose   I _____ not to go when I saw who was going.
7. lie   Ned _____ down on the grass and took a nap.
8. carry   Michael _____ the box to the grocery store.
9. take   Mom _____ me to the movies.
10. mow   My dad _____ the grass today.
11. give   Maria _____ John the bicycle.
12. win   We _____ the game last night.
13. listen   The children _____ to the radio.
14. dance   The ballerina _____ on the stage.
15. dress   Larry _____ the children for school.
16. throw   The man _____ the bottle in the water.
17. eat   The couple _____ the pizza for dinner.
18. watch   My father and I _____ television yesterday.
19. pull   The dog _____ the wagon into the yard.
20. sing   The church choir _____ in the Christmas program.
21. wait   The children _____ for the school bus.

Copyright © 1987 LinguiSystems, Inc.

22. laugh   Barbara _____ at the circus clowns.

23. stand   Jan _____ at the front door.

24. sleep   She _____ until noon yesterday.

25. cry   The baby _____ when he was hungry.

26. forget   I _____ to keep my appointment with the doctor.

27. sit   The school children _____ in their desks.

28. draw   Jay _____ a beautiful picture.

29. walk   I _____ home last night.

30. hold   He _____ his breath when he went underwater.

I.E.P. Goal: The client will use regular and irregular past tense verb forms in sentences with 90% or greater accuracy.

Grammar
Task AA: Choosing the Correct Sentence for Future Tense Verbs

Read the sets of sentences below. Put a check beside the sentence that tells something that will happen in the future. The first one is done for you.

1. ___ Marcia to go to the concert.
   ✓ Marcia will go to the concert.

2. ___ Cecile will like the play.
   ___ Cecile will liking the play.

3. ___ John will not go with me tonight.
   ___ John will not went with me tonight.

4. ___ The fortune teller will told your fortune.
   ___ The fortune teller will tell your fortune.

5. ___ The children will work hard on the pageant.
   ___ The children will to work hard on the pageant.

6. ___ The neighbors are not to going to the potluck dinner.
   ___ The neighbors will not go to the potluck dinner.

7. ___ Will you help me with my homework?
   ___ Will you helping me with my homework?

8. ___ Randy will fixed the television set for you.
   ___ Randy will fix the television set for you.

9. ___ The typewriter won't working tonight.
   ___ The typewriter will not work tonight.

10. ___ Marty will help drive the car home.
    ___ Marty will to help drive the car home.

11. ___ The air conditioner stopped cooling tomorrow.
    ___ The air conditioner will stop cooling tomorrow.

12. ___ The janitor will clean out the trash cans tonight.
    ___ The janitor clean out the trash cans tonight.

13. ___ Silver will tarnish if not cleaned properly.
    ___ Silver tarnished if not cleaned properly.

14. ___ The coffeemaker will to make enough coffee.
    ___ The coffeemaker will make enough coffee.

15. ___ The groom will say, "I do."
    ___ The groom to say, "I do."

16. ___ Michele knocked on the door when she gets here.
    ___ Michele will knock on the door when she gets here.

17. ___ The press ran out of ink the day after tomorrow.
    ___ The press will run out of ink the day after tomorrow.

18. ___ We will join them at the cabin later.
    ___ We joining them at the cabin later.

19. ___ The dog will to go to the kennel.
    ___ The dog will go to the kennel.

20. ___ The sun will came up tomorrow.
    ___ The sun will come up tomorrow.

21. ___ We will went to the beach.
    ___ We will go to the beach.

22. ___ It will rained this weekend.
    ___ It will rain this weekend.

23. ___ Terry will to watch the show.
    ___ Terry will watch the show.

24. ___ Harold will walk to the store later.
    ___ Harold will walked to the store.

25. ___ Jonathan will caught the ball.
    ___ Jonathan will catch the ball.

I.E.P. Goal: The client will identify future tense verb forms in sentences with 90% or greater accuracy.

Grammar

Task BB: Fill-in-the-Blank for Future Tense Verbs

The first sentence in each set describes something that has already happened or that is happening now. Fill in the blank in the second sentence to tell what will happen in the future. The first one is done for you.

1. Today I went to school.

   Tomorrow I __will__ __go__ to school.

2. Yesterday I lost my ring.

   I hope I _____ _____ it.

3. I am going out at seven o'clock.

   Tomorrow I _____ _____ out at eight o'clock.

4. This year I am in the third grade.

   Next year I _____ _____ in the fourth grade.

5. Last summer I worked at a camp.

   This summer I _____ _____ at a movie theater.

6. John got the job today.

   Tomorrow he _____ _____ to work.

7. Melanie walks to the store every day.

   Tomorrow she _____ _____ to the store.

8. Jeff starts the car before going to the store.

   Tomorrow he _____ _____ the car.

9. Ray watches TV a lot.

   Later, Ray _____ _____ a TV program.

10. The dentist cleans our teeth.

    He _____ _____ my teeth next week.

11. We played two games today.

    Next week we _____ _____ four games.

12. The clocked chimed the hour.

    Next hour the clock _____ _____ again.

13. Mark wants to go to the fair.

    Tomorrow he _____ _____ to the fair.

14. The carpet needs a cleaning.

    The maid _____ _____ it tomorrow.

15. The mechanic checked the oil level in the car.

    He _____ _____ it again tomorrow.

16. Mary visited me yesterday.

    She _____ _____ Beth tonight.

17. Peg moved to Roanoke this week.

    She _____ _____ to Richmond next year.

18. Barry was unable to reach the director on the phone.

    He _____ _____ her tomorrow.

19. Jerome never went skiing before.

    He _____ _____ skiing this summer.

20. Joe stayed at the bank all day giving instruction.

    Tomorrow he _____ _____ for three hours.

21. The mechanic repaired three cars today.

    Next week he _____ _____ the remaining cars in the garage.

22. The children went to the movies last Saturday.

    They _____ _____ next Saturday for the new feature.

23. The lumberjack chopped the trees down.

    This weekend he _____ _____ more trees down.

24. The baker put the icing on one birthday cake.

    Tomorrow he _____ _____ the icing on the rest of the cakes.

25. Today the weather is cloudy and damp.

    Tomorrow it _____ _____ hot and sunny.

26. The dog barked when he heard the noise.

    The dog _____ _____ when the neighbors come home.

27. The boy took a bath last night.

   The boy _____ _____ a bath again tonight.

28. The woman drove in from New Jersey yesterday.

   Tomorrow she _____ _____ to work.

29. The workmen stopped to eat lunch at noon today.

   Tomorrow they _____ _____ to eat lunch at noon.

30. The cotton shirt shrank in the hot dryer.

   The cotton pants _____ _____ in the dryer, too.

I.E.P. Goal: *The client will supply correct future tense verb forms in sentences with 90% or greater accuracy.*

Grammar
Task CC: Choosing the Correct Sentence with Mixed Verb Forms

Read each set of sentences below. Put a check beside the sentence in each set that is correct. The first one is done for you.

1. ___ Henry to go to camp next summer.
   ✓ Henry will go to camp next summer.

2. ___ The basketball sped through the air.
   ___ The basketball speeded through the air.

3. ___ The boys were running and the girl was following them.
   ___ The boys was running and the girl was following them.

4. ___ Have you ever wrote a story?
   ___ Have you ever written a story?

5. ___ Two scouts came to the meeting.
   ___ Two scouts come to the meeting.

6. ___ Did you gave it to him?
   ___ Did you give it to him?

7. ___ Will you teach me that song?
   ___ Will you taught me that song?

8. ___ She breaked her arm.
   ___ She broke her arm.

9. ___ When will you go to the movie?
   ___ When will you went to the movie?

10. ___ Matt scare the rabbit in the field yesterday.
    ___ Matt scared the rabbit in the field yesterday.

148

11. ___ I like to sits in the swing.
    ___ I like to sit in the swing.

12. ___ Phil plays the harmonica for me.
    ___ Phil will plays the harmonica for me.

13. ___ The car runs on unleaded fuel.
    ___ The car ranned on unleaded fuel.

14. ___ The children seed a big truck.
    ___ The children saw a big truck.

15. ___ Dad will mow the grass when he comes home.
    ___ Dad will mowed the grass when he comes home.

16. ___ My husband choosed the glasses he wanted.
    ___ My husband chose the glasses he wanted.

17. ___ Do you have a big house?
    ___ Do you had a big house?

18. ___ We goed on a long trip last year.
    ___ We went on a long trip last year.

19. ___ Leslie walked to the park tomorrow.
    ___ Leslie will walk to the park tomorrow.

20. ___ Is Margaret coming to the picnic?
    ___ Is Margaret come to the picnic?

21. ___ The boy is climbing the tree in the back.
    ___ The boy climbing the tree in the back.

22. ___ Janet made the peach preserves.
    ___ Janet make the peach preserves.

23. ___ The boy bended the wire.
    ___ The boy bent the wire.

24. ___ The police will not be here then.
    ___ The police will not been here then.

25. ___ The camp close down in the winter.
    ___ The camp closed down in the winter.

26. ___ The thief jam the door shut with a bar.
    ___ The thief jammed the door shut with a bar.

27. ___ Boxers hit sandbags to develop their hand strength.
    ___ Boxers is hit sandbags to develop their hand strength.

28. ___ The air conditioner run all day long.
    ___ The air conditioner ran all day long.

29. ___ Candy tastes sweet and is fun to eat.
    ___ Candy is tastes sweet and fun to eat.

30. ___ The rabbit hopped into the green field.
    ___ The rabbit to hop into the green field.

I.E.P. Goal: The client will identify grammatically correct verb tense forms within sentences with 90% or greater accuracy.

Grammar
Task DD: Fill-in-the-Blank for Mixed Verb Tenses

Complete each sentence with the correct form of the verb beside the sentence. Be sure your answer makes sense with the rest of the sentence. The first one is done for you.

1. go   Terry and Chip ___will go___ to the movie next week.

2. hit   I _____ a home run in the last game!

3. sing   Martha _____ in the Apple Blossom Festival last year.

4. sit   I like to _____ on the porch.

5. help   Please _____ me sit down.

6. play   The boys are _____ in the field next door.

7. give   Never _____ up before you try.

8. open   Sherry _____ the door for me earlier.

9. give   Dad _____ money to the March of Dimes next week.

10. want   I _____ a bicycle for my birthday, but I got a dress instead.

11. bury   The sailors _____ the treasure a hundred years ago.

12. walk   Sheila is _____ to school this week.

13. throw The catcher _____ the ball to the pitcher after the game was over.

14. come   Many people _____ to the carnival last night.

15. go   Are you _____ to the dance?

16. write He is _____ a book.

17. sit   The boy _____ on the floor to fix his bicycle.

18. fly   The birds _____ south when winter comes.
19. cry   I _____ when I am unhappy.
20. freeze   The water _____ in the lake last year.
21. like   Jim _____ to eat beef and chicken.
22. go   The children _____ to school tomorrow.
23. shovel   The miner _____ the coal into the pit last week.
24. teach   My sister _____ third grade last year.
25. write   Maria won't _____ the paper until later.
26. cook   Penny _____ dinner for her boyfriend later tonight.
27. listen   We _____ to the radio on our trip back from Ontario last week.
28. marry   Will you _____ me?
29. fall   Bob and Dean _____ down the hill yesterday afternoon.
30. get   Dad _____ the food at the store this weekend.

I.E.P. Goal: The client will use past, present, present progressive or future tense verbs in sentences with 90% or greater accuracy.

Grammar
Task EE: Generation of Verb Tenses

Write a short sentence for the present, past and future tenses of each verb. Use the phrases listed below. The first one is done for you.

1. buy   Today, I _buy_. Yesterday, I _bought_. Tomorrow, I _will buy_.
2. deliver Today, I _____. Yesterday, I _____. Tomorrow, I _____.
3. bring   Today, I _____. Yesterday, I _____. Tomorrow, I _____.
4. jump   Today, I _____. Yesterday, I _____. Tomorrow, I _____.
5. think   Today, I _____. Yesterday, I _____. Tomorrow, I _____.
6. knock   Today, I _____. Yesterday, I _____. Tomorrow, I _____.
7. shout   Today, I _____. Yesterday, I _____. Tomorrow, I _____.
8. speak   Today, I _____. Yesterday, I _____. Tomorrow, I _____.
9. dance   Today, I _____. Yesterday, I _____. Tomorrow, I _____.

10. ring   Today, I _____.   Yesterday, I _____.   Tomorrow, I _____.

11. wear   Today, I _____.   Yesterday, I _____.   Tomorrow, I _____.

12. fall   Today, I _____.   Yesterday, I _____.   Tomorrow, I _____.

13. catch   Today, I _____.   Yesterday, I _____.   Tomorrow, I _____.

14. reach   Today, I _____.   Yesterday, I _____.   Tomorrow, I _____.

15. joke   Today, I _____.   Yesterday, I _____.   Tomorrow, I _____.

16. mix   Today, I _____.   Yesterday, I _____.   Tomorrow, I _____.

17. draw   Today, I _____.   Yesterday, I _____.   Tomorrow, I _____.

18. find   Today, I _____.   Yesterday, I _____.   Tomorrow, I _____.

19. cook   Today, I _____.   Yesterday, I _____.   Tomorrow, I _____.

20. push   Today, I _____.   Yesterday, I _____.   Tomorrow, I _____.

21. lend   Today, I _____.   Yesterday, I _____.   Tomorrow, I _____.

22. forget   Today, I _____.   Yesterday, I _____.   Tomorrow, I _____.

23. get   Today, I _____.   Yesterday, I _____.   Tomorrow, I _____.

24. dig   Today, I _____.   Yesterday, I _____.   Tomorrow, I _____.

25. paint   Today, I _____.   Yesterday, I _____.   Tomorrow, I _____.

26. skate   Today, I _____.   Yesterday, I _____.   Tomorrow, I _____.

27. skip   Today, I _____.   Yesterday, I _____.   Tomorrow, I _____.

28. say   Today, I _____.   Yesterday, I _____.   Tomorrow, I _____.

29. love   Today, I _____.   Yesterday, I _____.   Tomorrow, I _____.

30. fix   Today, I _____.   Yesterday, I _____.   Tomorrow, I _____.

I.E.P. Goal: *The client will form the present, past, and future tenses of regular and irregular verbs in short sentences with 90% or greater accuracy.*

Grammar
Task FF: Rearranging Words to Form Correct and Complete Sentences

Rearrange the words to make a complete sentence. The first one is done for you.

1. to movies we went the

    We went to the movies.

2. saw many he things
_____.

3. go want don't I to
_____.

4. steep hill was it a
_____.

5. sick baby is my
_____.

6. beautiful bride was the
_____.

7. car New the Jersey Dad to drove
_____.

8. my birthday on Tuesday is
_____.

9. answer have the you
_____.

10. here in it's too noisy
_____.

11. hurry we all sometimes must
_____.

12. silently and softly the fell rain
_____.

13. want to go with us out do you
_____.

14. have fun we do school after
_____.

15. dress Melanie wore her blue new
_____.

16. to rattles babies play like with
    _____.

17. she downstairs went quickly
    _____.

18. the new red shiny is bike
    _____.

19. team won our the game
    _____.

20. pet I want really a
    _____.

21. jumped the doctor into his car
    _____.

22. sister Amy my dog has a
    _____.

23. the mowed grass man the green
    _____.

24. don't homework I understand my
    _____.

25. can't chair the sit on you porch the front on
    _____.

26. I my lost handkerchief theater in the
    _____.

27. peaceful in walking is the woods
    _____.

28. husband is my man a kind
    _____.

29. diving I the board jumped off
    _____.

30. boxes please the the shelf put on

_____.

I.E.P. Goal: The client will rearrange words to form grammatically and syntactically correct sentences with 90% or greater accuracy.

Grammar
Task GG: Description of Common Objects

Use complete sentences to describe how the following objects look. The first one is done for you.

1. a tree *It has a trunk, branches, and green leaves*.
2. a pencil _____.
3. a dog _____.
4. your television set _____.
5. your pajamas _____.
6. your tennis shoes _____.
7. your bedroom _____.
8. a watch _____.
9. your schoolroom _____.
10. a movie theater _____.
11. a Ferris wheel _____.
12. a zoo _____.
13. a washing machine _____.
14. a guitar _____.
15. a city street _____.
16. a car _____.
17. a swimming pool _____.
18. a desk _____.
19. a piece of gum _____.
20. a telephone pole _____.

21. a bicycle _____.
22. a shower _____.
23. a swing set _____.
24. a buckle _____.
25. a football stadium _____.
26. a river _____.
27. a driveway _____.
28. a ring _____.
29. a sailboat _____.
30. a tissue _____.
31. eyeglasses _____.
32. sandals _____.
33. a van _____.
34. a license plate _____.
35. a football _____.
36. a bus _____.
37. a cloud _____.
38. a bucket _____.
39. a stop sign _____.
40. a diaper _____.
41. a lawn mower _____.
42. a rubber band _____.
43. a daisy _____.
44. a cigar _____.
45. a shutter _____.
46. a flag _____.

47. a barn _____.

48. a chimney _____.

49. a razor _____.

50. a bed _____.

I.E.P. Goal: *The client will describe the appearance of given objects using complete sentences with 90% or greater accuracy.*

Note: Instruct the client to focus on the object's appearance and not its function. The appropriateness of the client's answer is left to the clinician's discretion.

Grammar
Task HH: Completion of Story Line

Add two or three sentences to each of the following of the stories listed below. The first one is done for you.

1. Yesterday my mother took us to the store.
   She gave us each a quarter to buy candy. I bought bubble gum with mine.

2. My grandmother could not find her glasses.
   _____
   _____

3. The girl ran screaming from the building.
   _____
   _____

4. My favorite time of the day is the evening.
   _____
   _____

5. It was so dark that I could not see my hand in front of my face. Then I heard something behind me.
   _____
   _____

6. The table was set and the guests had arrived.
   _____
   _____

7. My mother is the best cook I know. She can make anything.

8. The children went to the movies.

9. It was quiet and peaceful with the snow falling outside.

10. Kids love the summertime.

11. The woods were bright with the raging fire. Smoke could be seen for miles.

12. Baseball is an exciting sport.

13. On our trip to the zoo, we saw a lot of interesting things.

14. The alarm clock went off at four A.M. We were going fishing early.

15. A pet needs a lot of care.

16. On Saturday, Dad did all of his household chores.

17. The vegetables arrived at the grocery store. They were weighed and counted.

18. Have you ever been to an Indian reservation?

19. The man was caught speeding by the police officer.

20. The little boy was worried about his first day of school.

21. In the morning I must get ready for camp.

22. My garden is the prettiest on the block.

23. The color television set was brand new. I couldn't wait to watch my favorite shows.

24. I heard a dog whining in the back yard. When I looked out my window, I saw something brown and white near the fence.

25. A great deal of preparation goes into getting married.

_____

_____

I.E.P. Goal: *The client will add grammatically correct sentences to a story line with 90% or greater accuracy.*

Note: The appropriateness of the client's response is based on clinical judgement.

Grammar: General Activities

1. Ask the student to make a pronoun booklet using magazine pictures to depict nominative and objective pronouns (he, she, her, him, they, it). Then use the booklet for practice with sentence construction using pronouns. Have the student formulate a sentence for each picture.

2. To increase correct use of "I" in conversation during daily activities, ask the student questions which can be answered with initial "I" instead of yes/no. For example, instead of asking "Do you want to go outside?", ask "Who wants to go outside?" Encourage the student to answer "I do" instead of "me," modeling the desired response as necessary.

3. To increase carryover of past and future tense to conversation, begin each session (or day) by asking what the student did the previous day stressing *did* in your question (e.g., What *did* you do yesterday?). End each session (or day) by asking what the student will do tomorrow, stressing *will* in your question (e.g., What *will* you do tomorrow?). If the student experiences difficulty with this task, model an appropriate response for him/her, stressing verb endings and auxiliaries (e.g., Yesterday, I play*ed* ball and practic*ed* the piano. Tomorrow, I *will* go to visit my aunt.).

4. Paste magazine pictures depicting pronouns on index cards. Have the student sort the pictures into appropriate stacks, boxes, envelopes, etc., which have been labeled with the appropriate pronoun. Then take the cards from each stack and have the student construct an appropriate sentence for each picture.

5. Photograph the student performing common activities (e.g., pushing, sitting, drinking, etc.). As the student looks at each picture of himself performing an activity, ask "What are you doing?" The student should answer "I am pushing," etc. You may also ask "Who is pushing?", and the student should answer "I am pushing." When the student can answer appropriately in response to questions, fade the question and instruct the student to tell about what he/she is doing in each picture.

6. Have each student act out a verb (one he thinks of or one you have whispered in his ear). Ask another student to tell you what the child is doing, using present progressive verbs. You may have to cue the child with a question (e.g., What is Joe doing? - "Joe is kneeling.").

7. Use several pictures from a magazine to make up a nonsensical story. Cue the student to use certain syntactical forms by asking key questions (e.g., What will the boy do?, Where had the girl been?, Who is in the house?) As the student tells the story, repeat all utterances after him correcting grammatical errors as necessary.

8. Using various common objects, have the student pick one from the pile and present it to a neighbor. The student then generates the sentence, "Now, the pencil belongs to

her/him." Another student is asked to generate another sentence about ownership: "The pencil is *hers/his*," or "The pencil is *Mary's*." A model may be needed until the students are familiar with the format.

9. Plurals: Generate cards depicting singular nouns and their matching plural nouns (box - boxes). Shuffle the cards and deal them out to each student (5-7 to each). Place the remainder in the middle of the table as a deck. The first student to the left of the dealer begins play by asking another student for a matching card to one he holds in his hand. He is to request the card using a sentence and the correct singular or plural form. For example, Jake has a picture of three geese in his hand. He asks another student "Do you have a goose?". Or if he had a goose in his hand, he would ask "Do you have any geese?". If the other student has the requested card, he must give it to the one requesting it and the student goes again. If not, the student picks a card from a pile, and it is the next person's turn. Play continues until all the deck is exhausted and all pairs have been matched. The one with the most matches wins.

10. Provide pictures of nouns described with regular and irregular adjectives (big, little, good, dirty, sick, etc.). Divide them into three piles - regular (*big*), comparative (*bigger*) and superlative (*biggest*). Place a student in charge of each pile. The regular form person begins by generating a sentence to describe his/her picture. (e.g., My house is *big*.) The comparative person holds up his/her picture and adds the comparative form: "My house is *bigger*." The superlative person would then complete the drill with "My house is the *biggest*." Once all the cards have been done, the students should switch the cards and begin again.

References

Bush, W. J. and Giles, M. T. *Aids to Psycholinguistic Teaching.* Columbus, OH: Charles E. Merrill Publishing Company, 1969.

Colin, D., Fillmer, H. T., Lefcourt, A. and Thompson, N. C. *Our Language Today.* New York, NY: Litton Educational Publishing, Inc., 1970.

Keith, R. L. *Speech and Language Rehabilitation.* Danville, IL: Interstate Printers and Publishers, Inc., 1972.

Kilpatrick, K. and Jones, C. *Therapy Guide for Adults with Language and Speech Disorders: A Selection of Stimulation Materials.* Akron, OH: Visiting Nurse Service of Summit County, 1977.

Novakovich, H. and Zoslow, S. *Target on Language.* Bethesda, MD: Christ Church Child Center, 1973.

Rosner, J. *Helping Children Overcome Learning Difficulties.* New York, NY: Walker and Company, 1979.

Stryker, S. *Speech After Stroke.* Springfield, IL: Charles C. Thomas, 1978.

Turner, D. R. *Miller Analogies Test - 1400 Analogy Questions.* New York, NY: Arco Publishing Company, 1973.

Van Hattum, R. J. *Developmental Language Programming for the Retarded.* Boston, MA: Allyn and Bacon, Inc., 1979.

ANSWER KEY

Specific Word Finding

Task A page 8

1. open, answer, shut
2. turn on, turn off
3. eat, fix, cook
4. drive, park, buy
5. tell, read, listen to
6. turn on, turn off, turn up
7. play
8. bake, make
9. sweep
10. build
11. rake, burn
12. clap, wash, fold
13. read, check out
14. tie
15. mail, write, send
16. close, cover, open
17. put on, tie, shine
18. water
19. drink, make, order
20. brush, comb, wash, cut
21. throw, kick, bounce
22. wipe, stamp
23. fly
24. catch
25. answer
26. blow
27. fly, land
28. climb
29. build, put out, light
30. tie
31. watch, go to
32. ride
33. wrap, open
34. take out
35. blow
36. climb
37. mow
38. climb, go up, walk down
39. buckle, tighten
40. inflate, blow up, pop
41. make, answer
42. sow, plant
43. pull, lower, raise
44. pay
45. take, pass, fail
46. pass
47. strike, light
48. take
49. answer
50. knit
51. take, go for
52. deal, shuffle
53. fix
54. run, win
55. follow
56. fluff
57. cash, write, bounce
58. direct
59. obey, break
60. give, follow
61. pour, mix
62. make, drink
63. tell
64. sift
65. recite, compose
66. seek, give
67. read
68. make
69. give, state
70. debate, decide

Task B page 9

1. shoes, glasses, pants
2. bread
3. cake, toast, candy
4. soda, milk, beer
5. water, milk, juice
6. water, milk, soda
7. groceries, potato chips
8. leaves, books
9. sugar, vanilla
10. soup, beans
11. water, rain
12. sugar, coffee
13. milk, gasoline
14. cereal, ice cream
15. toothpaste, glue
16. grapes, bananas
17. eggs, cigarettes
18. gum, wolves
19. coffee, tea
20. soup, cereal
21. cereal, crackers
22. laundry, wood, coal
23. milk, oil
24. snow, soap
25. butter, bacon, hamburger
26. cookies, hot dogs
27. cloth, ribbon
28. lettuce, cabbage
29. bees, insects
30. eggs, doughnuts
31. coal, sugar
32. soap, gold
33. gum, butter, margarine
34. jelly, pickles
35. celery
36. people, friends
37. lemonade, beer, water
38. soap, yeast
39. sticks, laundry, rags
40. baking powder, vanilla, flour
41. meat, cookies
42. clothes
43. medicine
44. Indians
45. coffee, nails
46. apples, potatoes
47. roses
48. potatoes, oats
49. gold
50. matches, verse
51. pins, letters
52. geese, sheep
53. beef
54. power, electricity

Task C page 10

1. hands
2. game, record
3. book
4. ball
5. light
6. song
7. letter
8. hair
9. door
10. bicycle, horse
11. picture
12. bell
13. house
14. paper
15. car
16. ball, cold
17. ladder
18. door
19. kite, airplane
20. picture
21. ball
22. pencil
23. food, clothes
24. boat
25. flowers, cherries
26. coat
27. hair
28. dog, cat
29. glass, leg
30. lawn
31. picture
32. story
33. meal, snack
34. rope
35. story, radio
36. nail
37. dishes, clothes
38. plants, flowers
39. trash
40. leg, arm
41. cake, drink
42. noise
43. table, counter
44. house, floor
45. homework
46. floor
47. money
48. wood
49. lamp, candle
50. check
51. wood
52. shoes
53. wood
54. clothes
55. race
56. letter
57. contest, race
58. package, gift
59. bill, fine
60. clock
61. cow
62. floor, car
63. picture, wash
64. cake, drink
65. directions, the leader
66. chicken
67. tambourine, bottle
68. ditch, hole
69. flour
70. cake, room
71. book, job
72. cut, wound
73. butter
74. parade, song
75. drapes
76. wood
77. ball, game
78. guitar, banjo
79. car, shoes
80. beans, vegetables
81. law
82. President
83. pants
84. spaghetti, juice
85. eggs
86. papers, folders
87. suspect
88. train, bus
89. money
90. crime
91. roast, turkey
92. balloon, inner tube
93. garden, plants
94. disease, sick person
95. numbers, figures
96. checkbook
97. motor, instrument
98. camera
99. stream
100. song, poem

Task D page 12

1. jelly
2. tell
3. Dad
4. water
5. boo
6. syrup
7. mouse, dog
8. comb
9. kiss
10. box
11. mustard, chili
12. king
13. men
14. pepper
15. treat
16. towel
17. night
18. **bat, chain**
19. lightning
20. **tomatoes**
21. dry
22. boys
23. meatballs
24. failed, true
25. bucket
26. gone, buried
27. slippers, pajamas
28. potatoes, vegetables
29. dryer
30. coast
31. not
32. fork
33. contents
34. key
35. week
36. brother
37. law
38. crime
39. mind
40. arrow
41. roll
42. Independence
43. Liberty
44. peace
45. entering
46. listen
47. thin, juicy
48. jump
49. Rights
50. never
51. swim
52. flowers
53. take
54. tired
55. board
56. weight
57. tackle
58. grass
59. easy
60. valley
61. crop
62. litter

164

Copyright © 1987 LinguiSystems, Inc.

ANSWER KEY

63. fancy, simple
64. sugar
65. borrow
66. dandy
67. ready
68. hand
69. dale
70. games
71. staff
72. battery
73. dried
74. press
75. error
76. soda
77. way
78. law
79. invigorating
80. hearty

Task E page 14

1. month
2. sandwich
3. machine
4. oven
5. board
6. chair
7. store
8. o'clock
9. roof
10. rain
11. puppies
12. restaurant
13. peel
14. dollar
15. ticket
16. wheel
17. register
18. stop
19. light
20. sister
21. cleaner
22. ears
23. pad
24. curtain
25. band
26. space
27. tracks
28. tooth
29. glasses
30. salad
31. chips
32. tire
33. sink
34. straight
35. tent
36. boil, whistle
37. errors, runs
38. grill
39. siren
40. cushion
41. license
42. plugs
43. box
44. drive
45. tip
46. stadium
47. tax
48. cloth
49. station
50. aisle
51. election
52. cooker
53. order
54. goal

55. club
56. percent
57. border
58. wagons
59. loft
60. country
61. prescription
62. chest
63. saw
64. powder
65. Testament
66. rights
67. Court
68. arrest
69. metal
70. cocoon
71. England
72. figure, shape
73. house
74. colors
75. tide

Task F page 17

1. toys
2. tire, steering wheel
3. cars, trucks
4. **paper**
5. bed
6. television
7. moon, sun
8. telephone
9. scissors
10. newspaper
11. shampoo
12. bib
13. mailbox
14. door
15. fan
16. soap
17. window
18. kitchen
19. razor, shaver
20. envelope
21. eraser
22. leash
23. square, rectangle
24. wallet, billfold
25. coffee cup
26. ashtrays
27. elevator, escalator
28. medicine
29. clothespins
30. checkers
31. dressing
32. jail, prison
33. permanent
34. dictionary
35. hive
36. island
37. furniture
38. hydrant
39. corner
40. suds, lather
41. lasso
42. flock
43. globe
44. history
45. atlas
46. telescope
47. jack
48. orphan
49. guarantee
50. hurricane
51. census

52. shingles
53. antique
54. fraternity
55. notary

Task G page 19

1. pencil, crayon, paper
2. stamp
3. plate, glass, silverware, napkin
4. soap, washcloth, towel, water
5. hammer, nail
6. wood, matches
7. eggs, butter, skillet, spatula
8. iron, ironing board
9. match
10. cake mix, eggs, cake pans, oven
11. keys
12. bread, toaster
13. fishing pole, bait
14. washing machine, detergent, dryer
15. snow, twigs, hat
16. seeds, trowel, tiller, water
17. invitations, decorations, guests, food, prizes
18. pajamas, toothbrush, clothing
19. shampoo, water
20. pumpkin, knife
21. lights, balls, tinsel
22. needle, thread, scissors
23. racquet, tennis balls
24. raincoat, umbrella
25. jack, spare tire
26. yarn, knitting needles
27. tent, sleeping bag, lantern, food
28. wood, saw, nails
29. camera, film
30. life preserver, inner tube, raft
31. batteries
32. paper, sticks, glue, string
33. pattern, cloth, pins, scissors, thread, sewing machine
34. leash
35. scale
36. hard boiled eggs, dye, cups
37. yardstick
38. fruit, sugar, water, jars
39. bleach
40. dictionary
41. fertilizer
42. turpentine
43. an offering, money
44. tanks, goggles, fins
45. washer, wrench
46. the fuse
47. sap
48. directions, map
49. the majority of the votes
50. antifreeze
51. compass
52. aspirin
53. microphone, speaker
54. stethoscope
55. propeller
56. tweezers
57. yeast

58. wool, spinning wheel
59. passport
60. truce, treaty, surrender

Task H page 22

1. mouse
2. bee
3. ice
4. pie
5. fox
6. mule
7. bird
8. flash, wink
9. glass, a bell
10. kitten
11. whistle
12. gold
13. molasses
14. night
15. silk
16. hornet
17. rail
18. fiddle
19. rock
20. arrow
21. cucumber
22. hills
23. picture
24. punch
25. kite
26. lamb
27. clam, lark
28. ape
29. feather
30. nails
31. life
32. ox
33. tack
34. rain
35. daisy

Task I page 22

1. face
2. cookie
3. hatch
4. lose
5. blessings
6. days
7. practice
8. glove
9. old fool
10. go
11. care
12. earned
13. candy
14. son
15. haste
16. early bird
17. flock together
18. saves nine
19. leap
20. grass
21. best man
22. sun shines
23. cooks
24. experience
25. honesty
26. free
27. candle
28. Friday
29. parade
30. straight
31. mind

ANSWER KEY

32. words
33. make it drink
34. new tricks
35. buck

Categorization

Task A page 28

1. lime, lemon, strawberry
2. turkey, ham, fish
3. ear, elbow, hand
4. coat, shirt, boot
5. flag, pencil, teacher
6. airplane, balloon, bee
7. frost, ice cream, icicle
8. toaster, light bulb, boiling water
9. Coke, cocoa, wine
10. doughnut, ring, wheel
11. cookies, Jell-O, sundae
12. bear, giraffe, chicken
13. swings, ball, hopscotch
14. anvil, concrete block, weights
15. couch, dresser, desk
16. popcorn, peanuts, pizza
17. screwdriver, wrench, drill
18. clam, shrimp, shark
19. cuff links, watch, earrings
20. ball, racquet, skis
21. Robert, David, Phillip
22. Emily, Alice, Wendy
23. Taft, Wheeler, Carter
24. California, Virginia, Maine
25. bus, train, bicycle
26. Wednesday, Sunday, Thursday
27. April, July, May
28. bleach, juice, coffee
29. thermometer, splint, pills
30. piano, violin, organ
31. "Star Spangled Banner," "Happy Birthday to You," "Jingle Bells"
32. gifts, games, prizes
33. mosquito, cricket, fly
34. peas, onion, spinach
35. bowl, basket, suitcase
36. peanut, pecan, hickory
37. bibs, rattle, bonnet
38. mittens, boots, ears
39. rose, daisy, poppy
40. hail, sunshine, hurricane
41. cap, helmet, derby
42. blueberry, chocolate, peppermint
43. Ford, Dodge, Volkswagen
44. bluejay, mockingbird, owl
45. arithmetic, English, science
46. razor blades, eyedrops, pills
47. Christmas, Labor Day, Chanukah
48. teacher, doctor, waitress
49. daffodil, butter, sun
50. taffy, rubber, bubble gum
51. circle, triangle, heart
52. roast beef, bologna, tuna fish
53. pop, pow, bang
54. crawl, leap, slide
55. Mercury, Pluto, Saturn
56. movie, opera, show
57. checkers, backgammon, Scrabble
58. fish, spades, canasta
59. Spain, England, France
60. Washington, Adams, Nixon
61. tent, backpack, compass
62. diamond, topaz, opal
63. sister, cousin, aunt
64. cinnamon, sage, paprika
65. axe, razor, wire cutters
66. brain, stomach, kidneys
67. taste, feel
68. tennis, shuffleboard, volleyball
69. lieutenant, major, general
70. birch, pine, hickory
71. Tooth Fairy, Jack Frost, Sandman
72. wheat, rye
73. Harvard, University of ___
74. mumps, flu, chicken pox
75. *Little Women, Nancy Drew, Moby Dick*
76. gold, silver, tin
77. Lutheran, Methodist, Episcopalian
78. Franklin, Whitney, Otis
79. tweed, wool, corduroy
80. electric mixer, food processor, juicer
81. queen, princess, earl
82. sword, pistol, saber
83. Gemini, Aquarius, Taurus
84. terrier, poodle, beagle
85. fox trot, cha-cha, break dancing, jitterbug

Task B page 31

1. colors
2. letters
3. numbers
4. toys
5. food
6. furniture
7. pets, animals
8. girls' names
9. boys' names
10. dogs' names
11. things worn on the feet
12. playground equipment
13. family members
14. things that are smoked
15. animal sounds
16. things that write
17. candy
18. things associated with Halloween
19. nursery rhymes
20. things that fly
21. amusement park rides
22. clothing worn outside when it is cold
23. clothing worn by a woman
24. things that are read
25. holidays
26. occupations
27. transportation
28. breakfast cereals
29. house plants
30. team sports
31. things that give light
32. things that tell time
33. baby animals
34. things that are round
35. things that break
36. places where money is kept
37. flowers
38. things that ring
39. jungle animals
40. things that have wheels
41. things that go up and down
42. entertainment, things we turn on
43. buildings on a farm
44. parts of a house
45. things kept in a wallet
46. medicine
47. Christmas tree decorations
48. things that can be tied
49. directions
50. liquids
51. birds
52. sewing materials
53. animals found in the ocean
54. months
55. things worn in the hair
56. makeup
57. languages
58. things that are green
59. window coverings
60. things that are worn around the neck
61. floor coverings
62. containers
63. times of day
64. building supplies
65. bed linens
66. people working in a hospital
67. things that have a pleasant odor
68. card games
69. cleaning supplies
70. things that have a point
71. stringed instruments
72. things used in riding a horse
73. dairy products
74. bodies of water
75. fasteners
76. places where we eat
77. condiments; things put on a hamburger
78. things that explode
79. luncheon meat
80. things used to weigh/measure
81. body joints
82. answers given to questions
83. things that make objects appear larger
84. materials
85. criminals
86. U.S. cities
87. states
88. grains
89. fictional characters
90. appliances
91. colors of hair
92. things that are light
93. measurements of distance
94. officers
95. countries
96. branches of the armed forces
97. Indian tribes
98. singing ranges
99. people in the Bible
100. oceans

Task C page 35

1. A door is not used for writing.
2. A table is not read.
3. Green is not a toy.
4. A lamp is not an animal.
5. A coat is not transportaton.
6. A dog is not the name of a baby animal.
7. Salt is not a color.
8. Birthday is not the name of a day of the week.
9. Spinach is not a fruit.
10. Cheddar is not meat.
11. A crayon is not a beverage.
12. A banana is not a vegetable.
13. A date is not a number.
14. A brick does not melt.
15. George is not a girl's name.
16. A bowl is not furniture.
17. A dog is not a jungle animal.
18. A toaster is not ridden.
19. A thimble is not jewelry.
20. A pepper is not a snack.
21. Both is not a direction.
22. A spatula is not a tool.
23. A sponge is not sports equipment.
24. Cole slaw is not a dessert.
25. An eagle does not live in the ocean.
26. A tablecloth is not clothing.
27. An oven is not found in the bathroom.
28. A snake is not an insect.
29. Gardening is not taught in school.
30. Saturday is not a holiday.
31. A valise is not a musical instrument.
32. An ear is not part of the leg.
33. A notebook is not made of cloth.
34. Perfume is not used for marking.
35. A belt is not worn on the head.
36. A horse does not fly.
37. Poison ivy is not a flower.
38. A child is not an occupation.
39. A cloud is not an action.
40. A chain cannot be tied.
41. Saltines are not a cereal.
42. You cannot see through a mirror.
43. A see-saw is not an amusement park ride.
44. A jukebox is not found in an office.

ANSWER KEY

45. Glue is not a cleaning supply.
46. A helmet is not used by a baby.
47. A cash register is not found in a schoolroom.
48. Vinegar is not a flavor of ice cream.
49. An astronaut is not a game.
50. A temple is not a shape.
51. An anchor does not float.
52. Concrete is not soft.
53. Grapes are not yellow.
54. A television is not found out-of-doors.
55. A book is not listened to.
56. Wednesday is not a month.
57. A tractor is not an appliance.
58. A dance is not a sense.
59. A bathtub is not camping equipment.
60. A snake does not have legs.
61. A neighbor is not a relative.
62. A zebra is not a farm animal.
63. Chicago is not a state.
64. A house is not small/round.
65. Mustard is not a dairy product.
66. Dirt is not a liquid.
67. An axe is not found at a party.
68. A rug is not made of metal.
69. A club is not a container.
70. A magazine is not one of a pair.
71. Surfing is not a winter sport.
72. A balloon does not have corners.
73. A collie is not a bird.
74. A hawk is not a tree.
75. A cow is not found in the city.
76. A sewer is not found on a farm.
77. Mud does not rip.
78. An umbrella does not stretch.
79. Lettuce is not cooked before it is eaten.
80. Oatmeal is not a type of sandwich.
81. A pig is not striped.
82. A galley is not part of a train.
83. A cranberry is not a nut.
84. A Metro is not a planet.
85. A funnel does not hold liquid.
86. A jockey is not an officer.
87. Password is not a movie.
88. A Tango is not a religion.
89. A sprain is not contagious.
90. An individual is not a gathering of people.
91. A jury is not associated with singing.
92. Rubber is not a metal.
93. Erie is not a country.
94. A judge is not a leader/ruler of a country.
95. A glass is not opaque.
96. A muscle is not an organ.
97. An island cannot sail into it.
98. Mercury is not a gas.
99. The Nile is not a mountain range.
100. Endive is not a type of cheese.

WH-Questions

Task A   page 60

1. milk
2. teeth
3. wash
4. paste, glue
5. play with them
6. read them
7. spoon
8. heat
9. someone pulls them up
10. detergent, washing them
11. wind
12. heat
13. bricks
14. to keep the car in, to keep tools in
15. chase them
16. sing them
17. deliver them
18. wear it
19. gas
20. the paperboy delivers it
21. polish
22. a switch, someone turns it on
23. someone pedals it
24. water, sunshine
25. metal
26. large with wings and engines
27. prettily colored with petals, leaves, and a stem
28. amen
29. to jump on
30. to take the temperature
31. *h*
32. maps
33. hamburgers, steak, hot dogs
34. caution
35. returns to the person who threw it
36. a billion, two million, etc.
37. brown/black and white with a long tail
38. flour, coffee, sugar
39. twelve o'clock
40. Monday
41. December
42. fruit
43. butter
44. shoes rubbing your feet, a burn
45. to lead a horse
46. Spanish
47. to transport money
48. North America
49. a turkey, meat, cloth
50. hot, humid

Task B   page 62

1. children
2. doctor, nurse
3. teacher
4. police officer
5. clown
6. mail carrier
7. author
8. farmer
9. grandmother
10. aunt
11. plumber
12. operator
13. artist
14. preacher, priest
15. baby-sitter
16. garbage collector
17. newspaper carrier
18. neighbor
19. carpenter
20. landlord
21. flight attendant
22. adult, race car driver
23. principal
24. chief
25. baker
26. astronaut
27. secretary
28. ballerina
29. miner
30. custodian, janitor
31. electrician
32. beautician, hairdresser
33. mechanic
34. repair person
35. chef
36. groom
37. librarian
38. clerk
39. conductor
40. veterinarian
41. photographer
42. cousin
43. soldier
44. cobbler, shoe repair person
45. conductor
46. lawyer
47. jeweler
48. teller
49. architect
50. emigrant, refugee

Task C   page 64

1. in the refrigerator
2. at a hospital, in his/her office
3. grocery store
4. at the pool/lake/ocean/river
5. in a bank, in a wallet/purse
6. at the airport, in the sky
7. at a department store
8. in the closet, in the dresser
9. in the dining room/kitchen
10. in the medicine chest/cabinet
11. motel, hotel, campground
12. in the dirt, in an anthill
13. in the kitchen/bathroom
14. service station, garage
15. in the trunk, in the garage
16. in a circus
17. in trees
18. upstairs, in houses
19. church, synagogue
20. in an office, on a desk
21. in the White House
22. shoe repair shop
23. in a pond, in its shell
24. in the living room, in the music room, at church
25. in an igloo, in Alaska
26. in a nursery, in a baby's room
27. to the library
28. around their waist
29. in the vault
30. the ocean
31. in my chest
32. in Washington, D.C.
33. under the bed, in a secret place, etc.
34. the basement, refrigerator, etc.
35. in the trash can, in the garage
36. in an art gallery/museum
37. in orbit, in space
38. a forest, from trees
39. in caves
40. in stables
41. a coal mine
42. underground
43. in New York City
44. in Asia
45. in France
46. where it is very cold, in the Arctic
47. at the center of the earth, 0° latitude
48. at the dairy
49. in a lab
50. in the orchestra pit

Task D   page 66

1. when we are dirty, at night
2. in the morning
3. in the morning
4. at breakfast time
5. in the evening, at 6 o'clock
6. when the old tire is worn out/flat
7. when it is cold, when we go outside
8. when it is over
9. when we go under the water, when we have the hiccups
10. client should state month or month and day
11. when we want to get to the other side
12. after a meal
13. when it is hot
14. at Christmas

167

ANSWER KEY

15. when we are sick, when there has been an accident
16. when it does not work, when the old batteries are no longer good
17. when we go to sleep, when we are scared
18. after meals, before we go to bed
19. when we are going on a trip
20. at night
21. when we go to bed, when we leave a room
22. when it is low or empty
23. in the spring
24. in the summer, when it is warm
25. when we want to go out, when someone knocks
26. when our shoes are too small/worn out
27. in the evening
28. on the due date, when we're finished reading
29. Autumn
30. February 14th
31. St. Patrick's Day
32. in the evening
33. October 31st
34. March 20th or 21st
35. when it is red/ripe
36. in the fall, when the crops are ready
37. in winter, when it is very cold
38. at dawn
39. July 4th
40. in the afternoon
41. the last Thursday of November
42. December 31st
43. the first Monday in September
44. during a play, movie, game
45. 1492
46. at the end of the fourth quarter
47. when we are trying to be quiet
48. 1776
49. at the end of the day, at a military funeral
50. on New Year's Eve or New Year's Day

Task E page 68

1. to keep them warm
2. to get his hair cut
3. so it looks nice, to get the tangles out
4. to buy bread, cake
5. so people can see to drive at night
6. to keep our hands warm
7. a unicycle only has one wheel
8. to protect their feet
9. because we might get hit by a car
10. because it would melt
11. to learn
12. because we are hungry
13. so they will get a good grade, so they will learn something
14. so people can go in and out
15. so people can hold on and not fall
16. because it rings, to make a call
17. so we won't get our clothes wet
18. so we can put things in them
19. to keep out the cold air
20. to turn them on and off
21. to take something out of the oven, so we won't burn our hands
22. so we can put the buttons through them
23. because we are happy
24. because we are thirsty
25. to let the water out
26. because they hear a noise, because they are excited
27. so they won't get dirty, because they won't fit over our shoes
28. so they can chew
29. to keep us safe if we have an accident
30. so people will stay on their side of the road
31. so they won't fall out of bed
32. to let in fresh air, so we can see outside
33. because we can put them on by stretching them
34. to warn of their approach
35. so we can read the time
36. because they do not run on the highway, because wheels are not useful in the water
37. because the weather gets cooler
38. so they can close their eyes
39. so we can move them to cut
40. because they would not roll
41. in case we make a mistake
42. so we can put them on the turntable
43. so we can mail it
44. so we won't get our shoes wet
45. so we don't swallow water
46. so we don't waste energy
47. so we do not have an accident
48. because we do not need the lights when we are asleep
49. so it does not get too tall, so we can play in the yard
50. so it won't spoil

Task F page 70

1. slowly
2. quietly
3. put them in the dryer, hang them on the line
4. pedal it
5. the sky becomes dark and cloudy
6. we see flames, we see smoke
7. it looks flat, it makes a noise
8. we see ice on it, we see someone fall down
9. we see it, it leaks
10. we can feel it
11. the alarm clock rings, someone wakes us
12. our others are too small, our old socks have holes
13. put bread in the toaster
14. look in the mailbox
15. taste it
16. you can hear them
17. it burns out
18. it looks dirty, we spill something on it
19. when we are out of food
20. ask the person who cooked it, look to see if the food is done
21. the lights in the theater come on
22. it is not cold
23. they will not cut easily
24. the door will not open
25. we see tire tracks
26. it is wet and wrinkled
27. it has someone else's name on it
28. ask him, look in the directory
29. look at the television schedule
30. ask him, look at the label of his sweater
31. ask our parents, look at our birth certificate
32. they grow thick fur, they hibernate
33. we hear an announcement on the radio
34. look at the calendar
35. school begins, the weather gets cooler
36. the bell rings, the teacher dismisses class
37. the doors are unlocked and the lights are on
38. it stops running, the gauge is on empty
39. we feel it
40. read the directions or the recipe
41. look at the size in our old shoes, have our feet measured
42. walk, ride a bike, take a bus
43. turn down the corner, use a bookmark
44. it looks a different color
45. look on the map
46. we get weighed, our clothes are too tight
47. we see a sign, we see all the cars going in one direction
48. pass a driving test
49. we use mortar/cement
50. by using radar and instruments

Task G page 72

1. bracelet
2. go to the beach
3. church
4. astronaut
5. tunnel
6. bicycle
7. milk
8. rabbit
9. driftwood
10. roller
11. top
12. submarine
13. hairbrush
14. a straw
15. red
16. carburetor
17. red
18. wrench
19. pitcher
20. torn pants
21. stapler
22. white
23. right
24. a game
25. celery
26. desk
27. bathtub
28. backpack
29. surf
30. floor
31. bleach
32. instant coffee
33. candy
34. shoe
35. cat
36. pickle
37. blonde
38. chapter
39. licorice
40. raisin
41. tomahawk
42. cloth
43. a gallon jug
44. planet
45. baby
46. France
47. cow
48. Ben Franklin
49. square
50. shoe

Task H page 74

1. clean it up
2. go home and get it
3. spread it out to dry, get another one
4. run for shelter, cover up the food
5. lie down, take an aspirin
6. offer to pay for it
7. return it for the correct size

ANSWER KEY

8. pull it out of your shoe, put medicine on your foot, get a Tetanus shot
9. go to the dentist
10. sweep up the broken glass
11. have it repaired, read a book instead of watching TV
12. sew it
13. look for it, buy a new one
14. call for help, climb out the window
15. throw away any food that had spoiled
16. tell one person you could not go to his/hers, go to each for part of the time
17. walk it the rest of the way, get it repaired
18. stay away from it, call the power company
19. apologize to him/her, buy him/her a present
20. take your pants to the cleaners
21. apologize for disturbing the person, dial again
22. have another one made
23. dig it out
24. cook something else, go out to eat
25. explain to the teacher why you were late, stay after school
26. get out of the water immediately
27. say "no," tell your parents
28. brush it off, throw it away
29. have it repaired, buy another one
30. try to pull it down, climb the tree and get it
31. buy a new one, use your finger for a brush
32. clean it up, tell the person in charge
33. put ice on it, cut it out
34. ignore them, tell the teacher in charge
35. let it ring, get out and answer it
36. get the tweezers and pull it out
37. spray the garden
38. give each person a half
39. pay for it, tell the librarian
40. build a fire in the fireplace, get out extra blankets
41. walk for help, sit in the car and wait for help
42. call the operator
43. tell her she had made a mistake
44. call the police
45. walk the rest of the way, get the next bus
46. put in a new washer, call a plumber
47. throw them away
48. use a compass, shout for help
49. tell them you had heard it, laugh anyway
50. stop and go another way, clean off the bottom of your shoes

Task I page 77

1. in a bed; at night; because we are tired
2. in the morning, at six o'clock, at lunch time; in the kitchen, in the dining room; food
3. in the washing machine; when they are dirty; soap and water, detergent
4. when we are dirty, at night; because we are dirty; in the bathtub
5. in the living room, in the den; in the evening, after school; because it is fun, because we are bored
6. to cut the grass; during the day, when the grass is high; in the garage/shed
7. boys and girls; for fun, to get somewhere; on the street, to school
8. in a department store; when we are in a store, when we want to go up or down; so we do not have to walk up and down the stairs
9. nurse, doctor, mother or father; to tell if we have a fever; in the medicine chest
10. in the spring; outside, in the garden; because we want to grow flowers
11. a carpenter, a person who is building something; when we want to cut wood, when we are building something; at the hardware store
12. outside a house, on the porch; to put letters and mail in; the mail carrier
13. to climb to the top of something; a painter, a firefighter; when we are painting the house, when we need to get on the roof
14. on a house, on the roof; when we have a fire in the fireplace; so the smoke does not fill the house
15. name school; to learn; state time and/or days
16. in the bathroom, bedroom; so we can see ourselves; when we are combing our hair, dressing
17. a gardener, a person working in the yard; so that we do not have to carry water in buckets; when we are watering the lawn, washing the car
18. on a windy day; children; outside, in the sky, at the park
19. to scrub the floor; in the kitchen, bathroom; dip it in a bucket, scrub the floor
20. at the skating rink, at the pond; in the winter; a pair of ice skates
21. to boil water; in the kitchen; water
22. children; at the playground, in our yard; because they are fun
23. to tow a car that does not run; when our car has broken down; from the garage or service station
24. to pound nails in wood; a carpenter, builder, workman; in the workshop, toolbox
25. to draw a straight line, to measure; at school, when we are measuring something; wood, plastic
26. in the snow, on a mountain; because it is fun, to go down a mountain in the snow; sporting goods
27. when the sun is shining, when we are driving; so the sun won't glare in our eyes; over our eyes, to the beach, at the swimming pool
28. in the kitchen; to keep food fresh; perishable food
29. for pleasure, to get somewhere; a jockey; in a stable, barn
30. strain food; in the kitchen; a cook
31. in a courtroom; men and women; to decide if a person is guilty or innocent
32. beauty shop/barber shop; when our nails need to be cut; a manicurist, a beautician, ourself
33. on a dashboard, in a car; distance traveled by a vehicle; on a trip
34. to grind corn, wheat; a miller, a farmer; flour, cornmeal
35. in a museum, gallery; paintings, artifacts, coins; artist, sculptor, collector

Task J page 82

1. It is not liquid.
2. It has two layers. It has icing.
3. It is round.
4. It is not worn to keep us warm out-of-doors.
5. It covers our ankles.
6. They grow on our toes.
7. It is worn on a finger.
8. It has a motor. It does not have to be pedaled.
9. It is warmer.
10. It has a hole in it for thread.
11. It is not for sleeping. It is found in the living room.
12. It is real. It grows on our head.
13. It has bristles. It does not have teeth.
14. You keep clothing in it.
15. It is used in the water. It is used for skiing.
16. More than one family lives in an apartment. It is rented.
17. It is clear. It comes in more flavors and colors.
18. They do not cover the toes.
19. It is bigger. It is made of a different material. It is worth less.
20. It does not quack. It cannot fly over a long distance.
21. It has a place for a cup.
22. It is not used with water.
23. It is used by women.
24. It goes over the water.
25. It has to be struck.
26. It is paved. It has more traffic.
27. The players may not pick up the ball and run with it.
28. It doesn't have a hump.
29. They are worn directly on the eye.
30. It does not go through the paper.
31. It is not made from cream.
32. It is prettier. It is cultivated.
33. It is dried. It is brown.
34. It is striped. It is not spotted.
35. It is frozen.
36. The paper can be taken out and put back in.
37. They are not used on pipes.
38. It is worn on the body. It is safer.

ANSWER KEY

39. It is not eaten by the fish.
40. Its snout is shorter and blunter.
41. It is held under the chin when played. It is higher pitched.
42. It is flat, not round.
43. It is acted out on a stage.
44. It contains definitions, not lengthy articles.
45. It cannot be removed by the patient. It is worn longer.
46. It tells the direction one is headed, not wind direction.
47. It is on the side of the car. It is not made of chrome.
48. It will not hold dirt. It has a blade on the edge.
49. It has many floors. It is found in cities, not along highways.
50. He preaches in a church.
51. It is nonfiction.
52. It is sour. It must be made.
53. It is given for chores and not for employment. It is less money.
54. It is not on the ground floor.
55. It deals with plants and animals rather than events.
56. It is not as strong. It is lighter.
57. It only has one hole in it.
58. It does not have to be done.
59. It is done in memory of a person or an event.
60. It carries blood back to the heart.

Task K page 85

I.
1. What do we wear on our heads?
2. What do we sing?
3. What do we use to brush our teeth?
4. What animal can fly?
5. What time do most children go to bed?
6. What number comes after three?
7. What month is the last month of the year?
8. What do we put on hot dogs?
9. What do we put on our car in the winter?
10. What can we hear?

II.
1. Who brings toys at Christmas?
2. Who flies an airplane?
3. Who goes to school?
4. Who has children?
5. Who watches over swimmers at a pool?
6. Who rides a plane, train, or car?
7. Who shows us to our seat at a play or movie?
8. Who gives a party?
9. Who participates in sports?
10. Who holds the highest office in a state?

III.
1. Where do people live?
2. Where do we keep food that might spoil?
3. Where do we wear a watch?
4. Where does our neighbor live?
5. Where do we put a tablecloth?
6. Where do we keep our driver's license?
7. Where do we bake a cake?
8. Where might we find a drain?
9. Where do we take suits to be cleaned?
10. Where do children learn math?

IV.
1. When is midnight?
2. When are cartoons on television?
3. When is summer?
4. When does it get dark?
5. When do we turn on the heat?
6. When do we rest?
7. When do we eat dinner?
8. When does the sun rise?
9. When is April Fool's Day?
10. When do frogs read?

V.
1. Why do we take an umbrella?
2. Why do we turn on the light?
3. Why don't we pick up a car?
4. Why can't elephants fly?
5. Why do we put ice cream in the freezer?
6. Why do some people wear glasses?
7. Why do we look at a clock?
8. Why don't we hit a balloon with a sharp stick?
9. Why do we sharpen a pencil?
10. Why do people riding motorcycles wear helmets?

VI.
1. What time is school over?
2. Why do we turn on the air conditioner?
3. What do we read?
4. Where do we keep our shoes?
5. What is a good drink?
6. Who calls strikes at a baseball game?
7. When is the weekend?
8. Who cries and wears diapers?
9. Where do sharks live?
10. Why do we carry spare tires in the trunk?
11. Where are criminals sent?
12. What do we do with a guitar/flower?
13. Where do we tie up a boat?
14. When do we frown?
15. Why don't we let children use sharp knives?
16. Who is a queen's husband?
17. Who is faster than a speeding bullet?
18. What animal's fur is used in making coats?
19. Who wore a glass slipper?
20. Why don't we eat steak everyday?
21. What color are grapes?
22. When do we pitch a tent?
23. Why do we oil a door?
24. Who discovered America?
25. What is our national bird?
26. Where is a prescription filled?
27. Where does cactus grow?
28. Who made the first American flag?
29. What is a cigarette made from?
30. Who invented the light bulb?
31. Why must cut flowers be kept in water?
32. Why are cards shuffled?
33. What keeps beverages hot or cold?
34. Where do nuns live?
35. Where are bells found?
36. When do we receive the newspaper?
37. What is used to hold back water?
38. Where are telescopes found?
39. When is there much unemployment?
40. What is the framework of a body?

GRAMMAR

Task A page 95

1. She
2. He
3. She
4. They
5. It
6. her
7. us
8. We
9. I
10. them
11. He
12. me
13. I
14. I
15. her
16. He
17. him
18. them
19. We
20. us
21. She
22. them
23. I
24. me
25. them
26. us
27. her
28. me
29. They
30. He

Task B page 96

1. He
2. she
3. her
4. him
5. She
6. He
7. They
8. them
9. We
10. He
11. him
12. us
13. We
14. They
15. us
16. them
17. They
18. She, him
19. her
20. They
21. She
22. He
23. her
24. They
25. us
26. He, her
27. We
28. them
29. her

Task C page 97

1. my
2. their
3. theirs
4. ours
5. her
6. yours
7. my
8. Our
9. his
10. his
11. his
12. My
13. our
14. Their
15. her
16. Her
17. Your
18. my, her
19. your
20. Her, mine
21. his
22. Their, my
23. her
24. their
25. our
26. him
27. their

ANSWER KEY

28. my, their
29. Her, my
30. our

Task D page 99

I.
1. him, his
2. her, hers
3. hers, her
4. them, theirs
5. his, him
6. her, hers
7. hers, her
8. him, his
9. hers, her
10. them, theirs
11. theirs, them
12. ours, us
13. her, hers
14. her, hers
15. theirs, them
16. us, ours
17. them, theirs
18. hers, her
19. them, theirs
20. his, him

II.
1. us
2. me
3. you
4. them
5. him
6. her
7. you
8. him
9. her
10. them
11. them
12. me
13. her
14. his
15. hers
16. theirs
17. ours
18. mine
19. yours
20. his
21. theirs
22. ours
23. yours
24. hers
25. mine
26. theirs
27. ours
28. his
29. yours
30. ours

Task E page 102

1. boy's
2. woman's
3. mother's
4. girl's
5. lady's
6. baby's
7. son's
8. sister's
9. rabbit's
10. child's
11. firefighter's
12. teacher's
13. hunter's
14. mail carrier's
15. neighbor's
16. David's
17. Becky's
18. Michael's
19. Mary's
20. Douglas'
21. Jeremy's
22. Zeke's
23. Mrs. Smith's
24. Theresa's
25. Andrew's
26. Joe's
27. Don's
28. Johnny's
29. Becky's
30. Linda's

Task F page 104

1. Tom is not sitting on the wall.
2. The door is not open.
3. Albert will not go to school tomorrow.
4. The car is not rolling down the hill.
5. Michael is not washing his car.
6. Johnny has not finished his work.
7. The ball has not popped.
8. The tree has not fallen down.
9. The paper carrier will not call tomorrow.
10. Santa Claus will not come on Christmas Day.
11. The girl did not jump into the lake.
12. Barbara did not part the girl's hair before rolling it.
13. The children have not gone to the circus.
14. Mindy may not go to the drugstore if she wishes.
15. He shall not have the position.
16. I would not have given some money for the project.
17. Daniel could not call for you.
18. Jimmy had not taken the boy to the doctor.
19. Linda and Emmy did not walk to the park.
20. The inheritance shall not be his.
21. You should not do the work yourself.
22. Ned did not hand the pipe to George.
23. I would not go if Mom let me.
24. Edward could not arrange for the room.
25. The tepee may not fall over in the rain.
26. The bookshelves could not be delivered today.
27. I have not heard about the job.
28. I should not go talk to her.
29. Ann had not driven the car to the lake.
30. The store has not sold one hundred copies of the book.

Task G page 105

1. couldn't
2. hasn't
3. shouldn't
4. haven't
5. wouldn't
6. won't
7. didn't
8. don't
9. doesn't
10. won't
11. can't
12. wasn't
13. wouldn't
14. couldn't
15. shouldn't
16. haven't
17. didn't
18. can't
19. won't
20. weren't
21. can't
22. hasn't
23. doesn't
24. wasn't
25. weren't

Task H page 107

1. bigger
2. smallest
3. farthest
4. sweetest
5. younger
6. sicker
7. poorest
8. finest
9. older
10. richer
11. fattest
12. widest
13. tallest
14. shorter
15. longest
16. wider
17. nicer
18. cheapest
19. prettiest
20. better
21. more
22. youngest
23. least
24. more
25. best
26. worse
27. most
28. more anxious
29. most
30. most appreciative

Task I page 108

1. bigger
   biggest
2. faster
   fastest
3. longer
   longest
4. smaller
   smallest
5. hotter
   hottest
6. nearer
   nearest
7. shorter
   shortest
8. smarter
   smartest
9. older
   oldest
10. colder
    coldest
11. cleaner
    cleanest
12. nicer
    nicest
13. taller
    tallest
14. wider
    widest
15. fatter
    fattest
16. richer
    richest
17. dirtier
    dirtiest
18. narrower
    narrowest
19. rougher
    roughest
20. wetter
    wettest
21. louder
    loudest
22. thicker
    thickest
23. slipperier
    slipperiest
24. stronger
    strongest
25. better
    best
26. worse
    worst
27. more
    most
28. more, less
    most, least
29. more handsome
    most handsome
30. more nutritious
    most nutritious

Task J page 110

1. dogs
2. hats
3. books
4. chairs
5. pencils
6. cans
7. apples
8. trees
9. rugs
10. pillows
11. skunks
12. schools
13. cars
14. clowns
15. guns
16. motorcycles

ANSWER KEY

17. bells
18. dolls
19. televisions
20. jars
21. dresses
22. cookies
23. gloves
24. cups
25. flowers
26. pens
27. cars
28. friends
29. bottles
30. stamps
31. bricks
32. pickles
33. doughnuts
34. potatoes
35. boxes
36. witches
37. lunches
38. churches
39. radishes
40. foxes
41. quizzes
42. houses
43. echoes
44. heroes
45. dishes
46. glasses
47. pearls
48. pretzels
49. eggs
50. potato chips
51. Lifesavers
52. jars of pickles
53. cans of soup
54. sisters-in-law
55. boxes of crackers
56. piles of leaves
57. stacks of papers
58. pocketfuls of money
59. bunches of bananas
60. brothers-in-law

Task K page 113

1. cookies
2. cake
3. beans
4. day
5. door
6. socks
7. eggs
8. drawers
9. lamp
10. teachers
11. chair
12. leg
13. flowers
14. pies
15. rug
16. bricks
17. stamps
18. doughnuts
19. books
20. cars
21. cans of soup
22. dresses
23. jar of pickles
24. television
25. potatoes
26. Witches
27. watch
28. crackers

29. friends
30. doughnuts
31. poles
32. stacks of papers
33. dish
34. game
35. bread
36. chairs
37. students
38. tree
39. rifles
40. pillows
41. days
42. Trampolines
43. roses
44. sisters-in-law
45. envelopes
46. typewriter
47. dunes
48. glasses
49. quiz
50. guns

Task L page 115

Word level

1. s, houses
2. s, buses
3. p, chair
4. p, player
5. s, legs
6. s, teachers
7. p, flower
8. s, doors
9. p, pencil
10. s, maps
11. p, apple
12. s, pickles
13. p, doughnut
14. p, cookie
15. p, pocket
16. p, box
17. s, bananas
18. p, watch
19. s, potatoes
20. s, quizzes
21. p, dish
22. p, glass
23. p, sock
24. s, sisters-in-law
25. p, pillow
26. s, piles of leaves
27. s, hoops
28. p, pearl
29. s, baskets
30. p, radish
31. s, desks
32. s, chests
33. p, basketball
34. p, trampoline
35. s, secretaries
36. p, gun
37. s, carpets
38. s, barrels
39. p, shirt
40. p, weed
41. p, finger
42. s, pictures
43. s, cups
44. s, crows
45. p, chicken
46. p, nose
47. p, belt
48. p, stereo

49. s, couches
50. p, fox

Sentence Level

1. p, witch
2. s, doors
3. p, doughnut
4. s, teachers
5. p, window
6. p, Hairstyle
7. s, carpenters
8. p, Glass
9. s, sisters-in-law
10. s, collections
11. p, Fox
12. s, loads of bricks
13. p, Television set
14. s, paintings
15. p, pickle
16. p, Stack of papers
17. p, Can of soup
18. s, dishes
19. p, lunch
20. p, Lifesaver
21. p, flower
22. p, Machine
23. p, Shrub
24. s, pocketfuls
25. s, piles of leaves
26. p, blanket
27. p, Clown
28. s, rocking chairs
29. p, bunch of bananas
30. s, couches

Task M page 117

1. feet
2. geese
3. mice
4. leaves
5. loaves
6. knives
7. wives
8. shelves
9. thieves
10. elves
11. roofs
12. chiefs
13. dwarfs
14. beliefs
15. scarfs or scarves
16. wolfs or wolves
17. calfs or calves
18. children
19. men
20. oxen
21. women
22. soap
23. deer
24. moose
25. sheep
26. fish
27. alumni
28. data
29. teeth
30. information

Task N page 119

1. foot
2. sheep
3. leaf
4. loaves

5. teeth
6. geese
7. knife
8. women
9. elves
10. roof
11. chiefs
12. moose
13. oxen
14. children
15. calf
16. fish
17. scarf
18. measles
19. ox
20. firemen
21. mathematics
22. dwarfs
23. wives
24. deer
25. bookshelves
26. mice
27. lives
28. deer
29. Moose
30. policemen
31. teeth
32. gentlemen
33. soap
34. sheep
35. Wolves
36. geese
37. Children
38. calf
39. feet
40. thieves

Task O page 121

Word Level

1. p, child
2. s or p, moose
3. p, mouse
4. p, tooth
5. s, oxen
6. p, foot
7. s, men
8. s or p, soap
9. s or p, sheep
10. s, elves
11. p, knife
12. p, leaf
13. s or p, information
14. p, woman
15. p, fireman
16. p, shelf
17. s or p, deer
18. s, loaves
19. s, wives
20. s, geese
21. p, scarf
22. s, thieves
23. s, roofs
24. p, wolf
25. s or p, fish
26. s, chiefs
27. p, belief
28. p, calf
29. s, data
30. s, alumni

Sentence Level

1. p, policeman
2. s, teeth

172

ANSWER KEY

3. p, deer
4. s, geese
5. p, leaf
6. p, wolf
7. s, sheep
8. s, knives
9. s, data
10. p, Ox
11. p, Woman
12. s, thieves
13. s or p, information
14. s, loaves
15. p, roof
16. p, alumnus
17. p, foot
18. s, calfs or calves
19. s, wives
20. s or p, soap
21. p, belief
22. p, mouse
23. p, Child
24. s, men
25. p, Fish
26. p, fireman
27. s, scarves
28. s, mailmen
29. s, moose
30. p, Elf

Task P page 123

Fill-in-the-Blank

1. pearls
2. players
3. horses
4. dolls
5. ox
6. candy bar
7. apples
8. geese
9. stamps
10. shelves
11. dresses
12. cans
13. chiefs
14. loaves
15. thieves

Discrimination - Mixed Forms

1. p, pie
2. p, woman
3. p, ox
4. s, potatoes
5. s, wives
6. s, fathers
7. p, window
8. s, chairs
9. s, doors
10. p, mouse
11. s or p, moose
12. s, houses
13. p, dress
14. p, policeman
15. p, goose
16. s, leaves
17. p, flower
18. s or p, sheep
19. p, shelf
20. s, feet
21. p, jet
22. p, sister-in-law
23. s, alumni
24. p, hero
25. s, wolves

26. s, cakes
27. p, branch
28. s or p, soap
29. s or p, fish
30. p, fireman

Sentences
1. p, friend
2. s, teeth
3. s or p, moose
4. **s, pencil sets**
5. p, child
6. p, leaf
7. s or p, deer
8. s, mice
9. p, scarf
10. s, houses
11. s, brothers-in-law
12. s, bunches
13. p, doughnut
14. p, belief
15. p, dish
16. s, men
17. p, elf
18. p, box
19. p, fish
20. s, dresses

Task Q page 125

1. are
2. was
3. were
4. has
5. were
6. is
7. was
8. are
9. were
10. has
11. was
12. is
13. have
14. are
15. are
16. Have
17. Are
18. is
19. are
20. walks
21. were
22. is
23. is
24. sleep
25. is
26. were
27. walks
28. was
29. are
30. was
31. was
32. does
33. were
34. is
35. was
36. are
37. is
38. likes
39. goes
40. does
41. does
42. have
43. was
44. is
45. have

46. have
47. have
48. has
49. have
50. does
51. fly
52. checks
53. ride
54. drives
55. waddle
56. write
57. hike
58. runs
59. reads
60. hit
61. are
62. Have
63. looks
64. are
65. wants
66. are
67. were
68. likes
69. calls
70. admits
71. opens
72. brings
73. assign
74. take
75. are

Task R page 128

1. The girl is walking to the store.
2. The boys are playing ball today.
3. The bird is falling out of the tree.
4. They are going to get caught if they aren't careful.
5. The cord is breaking with the strain.
6. Madeline is going to the concert tonight.
7. Marty and Joannie are having a party.
8. The juke box is playing old hit records.
9. Terry is not catching the ball.
10. The police officer is riding the motorcycle.
11. The building is burning.
12. The washing machine is washing the clothes.
13. The rocket is not falling from the sky.
14. She is reading the book.
15. Mark is missing his test tonight.
16. I am jumping into the pool.
17. The clock is ticking.
18. The temperature is falling.
19. Betsy is going to the beach today.
20. James is crying because he lost his dog.
21. The police officer is stopping the cars.
22. The boys are swimming in the pond.

23. The artist is painting the picture in his gallery.
24. The farmer is planting the seeds in his field.
25. The horse is neighing.

Task S page 130

1. is eating
2. is sewing
3. is jumping
4. is ringing
5. are singing
6. is walking
7. is hopping
8. is talking
9. is reading
10. is studying
11. is running
12. are talking
13. are driving
14. are crying
15. is thinking
16. are ringing
17. is writing
18. is flying
19. are selling
20. is watering
21. is burning
22. are marrying
23. is sleeping
24. are playing
25. is shooting
26. is typing
27. is jogging and swimming
28. is sailing and fishing
29. is laughing and playing
30. is typing and filing

Task T page 132

1. The boy walked home.
2. I washed the car.
3. She opened the letter.
4. The boys ate their lunch.
5. John helped me with my homework.
6. He pushed the door open.
7. He laughed at the story.
8. Bertha watched television.
9. The baby crawled up the steps.
10. The boy kicked the ball.
11. The children cried at the news.
12. The mothers talked about the children.
13. Penny jumped over the hurdle.
14. Michael shouted during the game.
15. The gentleman tipped his hat.
16. The salesclerk delivered the boxes yesterday.
17. Marcia jumped when she saw the spider.
18. The children skipped to school.
19. The ballerinas danced at the recital.
20. The school children waited for the bus.
21. The kitchen help cooked the dinner.

ANSWER KEY

22. We listened to the radio program yesterday.
23. Jeremy hopped on the green grass.
24. The firefighter saved the child.
25. Kevin crawled under the table.
26. Linda painted the window frame.
27. Dan pushed the wagon down the road.
28. Tom chewed the gum yesterday.
29. Paul swallowed pills with water.
30. Tim rested under the oak tree.

Task U   page 134

1. smiled
2. mowed
3. chopped
4. danced
5. laughed
6. waited
7. baked
8. skipped
9. looked
10. pushed
11. watched
12. jumped
13. rested
14. swallowed
15. chewed
16. crawled
17. opened
18. kicked
19. skated
20. worked
21. tripped
22. climbed
23. mixed
24. skinned
25. stopped
26. moved
27. washed
28. married
29. dropped
30. missed

Task V   page 136

1. asked
2. attached
3. bathed
4. carried
5. chopped
6. cleaned
7. climbed
8. cooked
9. crawled
10. cried
11. danced
12. docked
13. dropped
14. filled
15. fixed
16. gathered
17. guessed
18. hugged
19. joked
20. jumped
21. kicked

22. knocked
23. laughed
24. listened
25. loved
26. mailed
27. married
28. missed
29. mixed
30. moved
31. mowed
32. needed
33. nodded
34. packed
35. painted
36. peeked
37. picked
38. placed
39. played
40. pulled
41. pushed
42. raced
43. rained
44. raked
45. reached
46. remembered
47. seemed
48. shifted
49. shouted
50. sipped
51. skated
52. skimmed
53. skipped
54. smiled
55. smoked
56. sprayed
57. stayed
58. stopped
59. talked
60. teased
61. thanked
62. tipped
63. tripped
64. turned
65. voted
66. waited
67. walked
68. warned
69. washed
70. wasted
71. watched
72. waxed
73. worked
74. worried
75. zipped

Task W   page 138

1. Mary drank her chocolate milk.
2. The girls chose the costumes.
3. Michael drove the car.
4. The ice froze.
5. The window broke.
6. Jamie threw the ball.
7. The thieves stole the bicycle.
8. The model wore the pink dress.
9. The class wrote the play.
10. The children went on a field trip.
11. He gave to the United Way.
12. The boy grew three inches.

13. The teacher rang the bell.
14. He spoke for the children.
15. The bird flew away.
16. He drew the beautiful picture.
17. Gerald dug the hole.
18. The old man built the house.
19. Thomas sat in the chair.
20. The children blew the candles out.
21. Mick stood at the end of the aisle.
22. Betty ran down the street.
23. The squirrel broke the stick.
24. Amos slept all day long.
25. I awoke to the sound of popcorn.
26. I spoke to him about that.
27. The thief stole the car.
28. I brought it to you yesterday.
29. The pilot flew the airplane through the sky.
30. Larry gave her a ring last night.

Task X   page 140

1. hid
2. slept
3. fed
4. ran
5. bent
6. bought
7. ate
8. saw
9. threw
10. swam
11. won
12. wrote
13. spoke
14. drove
15. gave
16. began
17. flew
18. grew
19. stole
20. rang
21. broke
22. drew
23. ate
24. forgot
25. rose
26. lay
27. drank
28. slid
29. got
30. chose

Task Y   page 141

1. began
2. blew
3. broke
4. brought
5. built
6. bought
7. caught
8. chose
9. came
10. cut
11. dug
12. dove

13. did
14. drew
15. drank
16. drove
17. ate
18. fell
19. fed
20. felt
21. fought
22. found
23. flew
24. forgot
25. forgave
26. froze
27. got
28. gave
29. went
30. grew
31. had
32. hid
33. hit
34. held
35. kept
36. knew
37. led
38. leapt, leaped
39. left
40. lent
41. lay
42. made
43. met
44. read
45. rode
46. rang
47. rose
48. ran
49. said
50. saw
51. sold
52. shot
53. shrank
54. sang
55. sank
56. sat
57. spoke
58. spun
59. sprang
60. stood
61. stole
62. stank
63. swept
64. swam
65. took
66. taught
67. tore
68. told
69. thought
70. threw
71. wore
72. wove
73. won
74. wound
75. wrote

Task Z   page 143

1. forgot
2. gave
3. broke
4. cooked
5. crawled
6. chose
7. lay
8. carried
9. took

174

Copyright © 1987 LinguiSystems, Inc.

ANSWER KEY

10. mowed
11. gave
12. won
13. listened
14. danced
15. dressed
16. threw
17. ate
18. watched
19. pulled
20. sang
21. waited
22. laughed
23. stood
24. slept
25. cried
26. forgot
27. sat
28. drew
29. walked
30. held

Task AA page 144

1. Marcia will go to the concert.
2. Cecile will like the play.
3. John will not go with me tonight.
4. The fortune teller will tell your fortune.
5. The children will work hard on the pageant.
6. The neighbors will not go to the potluck dinner.
7. Will you help me with my homework?
8. Randy will fix the television set for you.
9. The typewriter will not work tonight.
10. Marty will help drive the car home.
11. The air conditioner will stop cooling tomorrow.
12. The janitor will clean out the trash cans tonight.
13. Silver will tarnish if not cleaned properly.
14. The coffeemaker will make enough coffee.
15. The groom will say, "I do."
16. Michele will knock on the door when she gets here.
17. The press will run out of ink the day after tomorrow.
18. We will join them at the cabin later.
19. The dog will go to the kennel.
20. The sun will come up tomorrow.
21. We will go to the beach.
22. It will rain this weekend.
23. Terry will watch the show.
24. Harold will walk to the store later.
25. Jonathan will catch the ball.

Task BB page 146

1. will go
2. will find
3. will go
4. will be
5. will work
6. will go
7. will walk
8. will start
9. will watch
10. will clean
11. will play
12. will chime
13. will go
14. will clean
15. will check
16. will visit
17. will move
18. will call
19. will go
20. will stay
21. will repair
22. will go
23. will chop
24. will put
25. will be
26. will bark
27. will take
28. will drive
29. will stop
30. will shrink

Task CC page 148

1. Henry will go to camp next summer.
2. The basketball sped through the air.
3. The boys were running and the girl was following them.
4. Have you ever written a story?
5. Two scouts came to the meeting.
6. Did you give it to him?
7. Will you teach me that song?
8. She broke her arm.
9. When will you go to the movie?
10. Matt scared the rabbit in the field yesterday.
11. I like to sit in the swing.
12. Phil plays the harmonica for me.
13. The car runs on unleaded fuel.
14. The children saw a big truck.
15. Dad will mow the grass when he comes home.
16. My husband chose the glasses he wanted.
17. Do you have a big house?
18. We went on a long trip last year.
19. Leslie will walk to the park tomorrow.
20. Is Margaret coming to the picnic?
21. The boy is climbing the tree in the back.
22. Janet made the peach preserves.
23. The boy bent the wire.
24. The police will not be here then.
25. The camp closed down in the winter.
26. The thief jammed the door shut with a bar.
27. Boxers hit sandbags to develop their hand strength.
28. The air conditioner ran all day long.
29. Candy tastes sweet and is fun to eat.
30. The rabbit hopped into the green field.

Task DD page 150

1. will go
2. hit
3. sang
4. sit
5. help
6. playing
7. give
8. opened
9. will give
10. wanted
11. buried
12. walking
13. threw
14. came
15. going
16. writing
17. sat
18. fly, will fly
19. cry, will cry
20. froze
21. likes, liked
22. will go, are going
23. shoveled
24. taught
25. write
26. will cook
27. listened
28. marry
29. fell
30. will get

Task EE page 151

1. buy, bought, will buy
2. deliver, delivered, will deliver
3. bring, brought, will bring
4. jump, jumped, will jump
5. think, thought, will think
6. knock, knocked, will knock
7. shout, shouted, will shout
8. speak, spoke, will speak
9. dance, danced, will dance
10. ring, rang, will ring
11. wear, wore, will wear
12. fall, fell, will fall
13. catch, caught, will catch
14. reach, reached, will reach
15. joke, joked, will joke
16. mix, mixed, will mix
17. draw, drew, will draw
18. find, found, will find
19. cook, cooked, will cook
20. push, pushed, will push
21. lend, lent, will lend
22. forget, forgot, will forget
23. get, got, will get
24. dig, dug, will dig
25. paint, painted, will paint
26. skate, skated, will skate
27. skip, skipped, will skip
28. say, said, will say
29. love, loved, will love
30. fix, fixed, will fix

Task FF page 152

1. We went to the movies.
2. He saw many things.
3. I don't want to go.
4. It was a steep hill.
5. My baby is sick.
6. The bride was beautiful.
7. Dad drove the car to New Jersey.
8. My birthday is on Tuesday.
9. You have the answer.
10. It's too noisy in here.
11. We all must hurry sometimes.
12. The rain fell silently and softly.
13. Do you want to go out with us?
14. We do have fun after school.
15. Melanie wore her new blue dress.
16. Babies like to play with rattles.
17. She went downstairs quickly.
18. The new red bike is shiny.
19. Our team won the game.
20. I really want a pet.
21. The doctor jumped into his car.
22. My sister, Amy, has a dog.
23. The man mowed the green grass.
24. I don't understand my homework.
25. You can't sit on the chair on the front porch.
26. I lost my handkerchief in the theatre.
27. Walking in the woods is peaceful.
28. My husband is a kind man.
29. I jumped off the diving board.
30. Please put the boxes on the shelf.

Task GG page 155

Accept appropriate responses.

Task HH page 157

Accept appropriate responses.